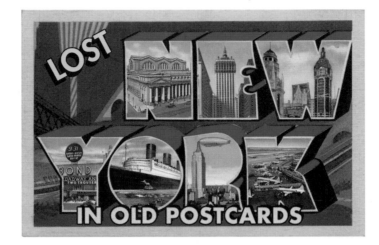

LOST NEW YORK IN OLD POSTCARDS

CREATED BY

ROD KENNEDY, JR.

WITH TEXT
& RESEARCH BY

ELIZABETH ELLIS

GIBBS·SMITH
P
PUBLISHER

SALT LAKE CITY

To the postcard guides, who always steer me in the right direction.

First Edition
05 04 03 02 01   5 4 3 2 1

Published by
Gibbs Smith, Publisher
P.O. Box 667
Layton, Utah 84041

Orders: (1-800) 748-5439
gibbs-smith.com

Edited by Suzanne Taylor
Designed by Steven R. Jerman—Jerman Design Incorporated, Salt Lake City, Utah
Printed by H & Y Printing Ltd in Hong Kong

Library of Congress Cataloging-in-Publication Data

Kennedy, Rod, 1944–
    Lost New York in old postcards / by Rod Kennedy, Jr. 1st ed.
       p. cm.
Includes bibliographical references.
    ISBN 1-58685-041-5
    1. New York (N.Y.)—History—1898–1951—Pictorial works. 2. New York—
(N.Y.) Buildings, structures, etc.—Pictorial works. 3. New York (N.Y.)—Social
life and customs—20th century—Pictorial works. 4. Postcards—New York
(State)—New York.
    I. Title.
F128.5 .K32 2001
974.7'1041—dc21
                                                                    2001001369

Acknowledgements

I am grateful this book was published and want to thank the following individuals and organizations for their help along the way:

Peter Simmons, former deputy director for collections access and publications at the Museum of the City of New York, who connected me with my publisher.

Elizabeth Ellis of the museum's collections access department, who did such a great job in writing the captions, for her help in gathering the research, and so much more.

Gibbs Smith, publisher, Suzanne Taylor, editor, and Steve Jerman, designer.

Jan Ramirez, formerly of the Museum of the City of New York, for her help and enthusiasm.

Grace Glueck, Lyn Stallworth, and Sharon Wendrow for their help with the proposal.

Judith Stonehill and Barbara Cohen of New York Bound Bookshop, which is now unfortunately a part of lost New York.

Martha Kaplan, my agent, for all her efforts on my behalf.

The Metropolitan Postcard Collectors Club and all the dealers who were a source for the cards.

The Curt Teich Postcard Archives and the Landmarks Preservation Commission for just being there.

Beverly Hegmann for putting up with it all.

Contents

9 INTRODUCTION

12 CHAPTER I:

East Side, West Side, All Around the Town

THE HARBOR

THE FINANCIAL DISTRICT

THE LOWER EAST SIDE

FLATIRON, CHELSEA,
    GREENWICH VILLAGE

PENN STATION,
    HERALD SQUARE

TIMES SQUARE

FIFTH AVENUE

ROCKEFELLER CENTER

THE EAST SIDE

CENTRAL PARK

THE WEST SIDE

HARLEM

52 CHAPTER 2: The Bronx, Brooklyn, Queens, and Staten Island, Too
    BRONX
    BROOKLYN
    QUEENS
    STATEN ISLAND

60 CHAPTER 3: Trip the Light Fantastic
    NIGHT LIFE
    RESTAURANTS
    THEATER
    SPORTS
    RECREATION
    SIGHTSEEING
    MUSEUMS

78 CHAPTER 4: Skyscrapers

82 CHAPTER 5: On the Go

86 CHAPTER 6: 1939 New York World's Fair

90 CHAPTER 7: Advertising Cards

95 CHAPTER 8: Special Effects
    ADD-ONS
    ARCHITECTURAL ANOMALIES

101 BIBLIOGRAPHY

103 INDEX

INTRODUCTION

Postcards have fascinated me for many years, but I became hooked when I started working on this project. It all started innocently enough one Sunday morning on my way to church. I was strolling through the flea market at 6th Avenue and 25th Street when I came upon a shoebox full of vintage New York City postcards. I was excited by the time-and-again, déjà vu feeling they evoked and by the fact that they pictured a colorful portrait of the city that no longer existed. Thinking this would make a great subject for a book, I began collecting postcards for a proposal. Little did I know what I was getting myself into, as it took six years to bring this project to fruition.

As my proposal turned into a collection and my collection into an obsession, I began looking for postcards every Sunday morning. I attended monthly meetings of the Metropolitan Postcard Collectors Club and went to the semiannual postcard bourse where more than sixty dealers and about a billion postcards are assembled in two grand ballrooms of the New Yorker Hotel. As if that wasn't enough, I began traveling to postcard shows throughout the metropolitan area and would even search out antiques dealers and flea markets on my vacations. I have even been known to frequent the ten-cent boxes at the postcard club meetings, getting down and dirty with all the other junkies.

The good news is that I sold the book (to pay for my habit), and in the process I have assembled a world-class collection of New York City postcards that I have donated to the Museum of the City of New York and some of which I am sharing with you in this book and exhibition.

Lost New York in Old Postcards documents the city from the turn of the century to the mid-1950s, the years in which hand-colored postcards were produced. These cards capture images of lost New York buildings, places, parks, hotels, subways, restaurants, nightclubs, theaters, and stores that no longer exist or have been transformed by the constant change defining New York as a work in progress. While we mourn the loss of such institutions as Penn Station and Ebbets Field, we are glad they are preserved in the collective subconscious of the place in the form of paintings, postcards, and photos.

Postcards are a synthesis of painting and photography, showing landmarks often embellished with tiny American flags, airplanes, beacons, and cloud formations that existed only in the artists' imaginations. These cards were gradually replaced in the 1950s, following Kodak's introduction of chromes (four-color process cards) in 1939. This book is meant to be as lighthearted and whimsical as the cards, with captions presenting unusual facts and tidbits of information about the images.

Postcards became popular after 1898, the year congress reduced the cost of mailing commercially printed cards from two cents to just a penny. Success was instant: Americans bought 770,500,000 cards in 1906 and just under one billion in 1913. Coincidentally, 1898 was the year New York became Greater New York, as a result of the consolidation of the five boroughs (Manhattan, Brooklyn, Staten Island, Queens, and the Bronx). All were now covered by the umbrella of a single municipal government. With the stroke of a pen, the population doubled to 3.4 million and New York became the second largest city in the world, topped only by London with four million. An unprecedented building boom ensued,

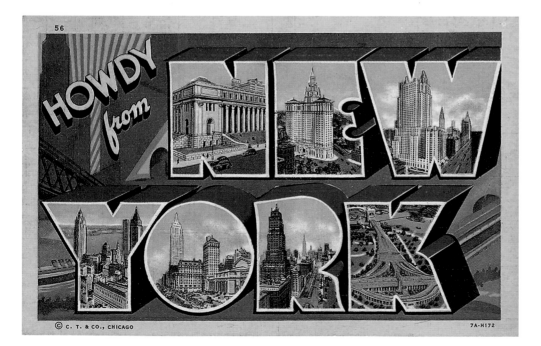

and over the next fifty years, the 284-foot-high steeple of Trinity Church, the tallest building in Manhattan in 1890, was surrounded and dwarfed by a vast metropolis of skyscrapers. Included in the boom were miles of subways, highways, bridges, and tunnels. Little old New York became the Big Apple, the greatest city in the world.

Fortunately, the popularity of postcards and the public's fascination with Gotham's many wonders coincided, and the city was endlessly documented in what many consider to be a miniature art form as well as an invaluable historical resource. Wrote famed photographer Walker Evans, "On their tinted surfaces are some of the truest visual records ever made of any period."

One final note: much like an Alfred Hitchcock movie, several of my friends and relatives make cameo appearances throughout the book. My grandfather, Franklin Kennedy, a Christian Scientist and a faithful churchgoer, was a look-alike for Frank Kennedy, the bartender pictured in the Piccadilly Circus Bar card on page 60. My great-great-great-grandfather, William Henry Craft, was one of the twelve people trampled to death shortly after the opening of the Brooklyn Bridge mentioned on page 78. Sidney Blackmer, featured in the Sweet Bird of Youth card on page 68, was a dear friend, as was Sigmund Halpern, founder of Futurama Printing, who named his company after the Futurama exhibit at the 1939–40 World's Fair mentioned on page 86.

Rod Kennedy Jr.

January 2001
New York City

EAST SIDE, WEST SIDE ALL AROUND THE TOWN

THE HARBOR

New York Harbor has been the gateway to this country since Giovanni da Verrazano sailed into it in 1524. Its deep waters, sheltered from the open ocean, make it a viable international port that is still the largest of these in the United States. This postcard depicts New York Harbor in the glory days of steamship travel. This scene would not be likely today, given the decline of luxury transatlantic steamships like the *Normandie, Queen Mary,* and *Queen Elizabeth;* immigration ships bringing new citizens to this country; and cargo ships that have moved to ports with larger space to handle containers.

America's Welcome, Statue of Liberty, New York Harbor

Detail:
Times Square at Night (with Kleenex)

"AT THE GATEWAY TO AMERICA"

© 1925 D. T. MAGOWAN, MAPLEWOOD, N. J. 14

U.S. IMMIGRATION STATION, ELLIS ISLAND

After 1892, when a ship carrying immigrant hopefuls to America docked at the piers along the Hudson or East Rivers, most first- and second-class passengers were given cursory inspections onboard before being allowed to enter the city. For those third-class and "steerage" passengers, however, another trip, this time by ferry, brought them to Ellis Island, where the process of becoming an American citizen began. Dormitories, kitchens, hospitals, laundries, and bathing facilities were built on the island to accommodate those whose status needed further investigation. By the time it closed in 1954, about fourteen million new residents had entered America via this portal.

THE STAR (NATIONAL AIRLINE)

Although Wilber Wright was the first person to fly within the boundaries of Manhattan in 1909 when he went from Governor's Island to Grant's Tomb during the Hudson-Fulton Celebration, National Airlines, a popular regional airline in the 1950s and 1960s, flew to Florida and then to Havana—at that time a weekend destination for New Yorkers. The entertainment newspapers of the time reviewed the shows and nightlife in Havana as they did for Paris and London. Visible below the plane in this card are a few of the numerous piers that once were used by cargo ships to bring goods to the city.

CHELSEA PIERS

The *Lusitania,* pictured here, was the first ship to land at Chelsea Piers before they were completed in 1910, and it was from here, in 1915, she sailed her last voyage; off the coast of Ireland she was torpedoed by a German submarine, killing almost 1,200 onboard. In 1912, the piers were also one of the possible docks for another ill-fated ocean liner, the *Titanic.* The *Carpathia,* carrying the survivors of this disaster, landed at Pier 54 on April 20, 1912. Chelsea Piers were closed in the late 1950s and subsequently were renovated and reopened as an athletic and entertainment complex.

Chelsea Piers, New York City.

BATTERY PARK AND LOWER MANHATTAN

This postcard gives a romantic view of lower Manhattan before the steel and glass skyscrapers of the financial district, Battery Park City, and the World Trade Center, which dominate today's skyline. When it was built in 1811, Battery Park's most notable feature, the circular Castle Clinton, was about 100 yards offshore. Originally a military fortification, it was converted to an entertainment hall and renamed Castle Garden in 1823. From 1855 to 1890, it served as an immigration center and then became an aquarium. Today, only the thick walls of the original fortification remain, and it is used for ticket sales to the Statue of Liberty and Ellis Island.

THE INTERIOR OF THE NEW YORK AQUARIUM, BATTERY PARK

The largest in the world when it opened in 1896, the New York Aquarium, in the refurbished Castle Clinton, quickly became one of the city's most popular tourist attractions. Housed in this facility were thousands of fish, some of which were brought back by local sea captains, hundreds of invertebrates, reptiles and amphibians, and several types of sea mammals. The aquarium also maintained a fish hatchery used to stock upstate rivers and supply schools with research specimens. It closed in 1942 under pressure to build the Brooklyn-Battery Tunnel, and, after a brief stint at the Bronx Zoo, it moved to Coney Island in 1957.

THE INTERIOR OF THE NEW YORK AQUARIUM, BATTERY PARK, NEW YORK CITY

The New York Stock Exchange, Trinity Church and Wall Street, New York City.

Copyright 1909 by Moses King.

STOCK EXCHANGE

Wall Street, named for the wall erected on it in 1653 by Peter Stuyvesant to protect the new city from invasion, has been a location of note for many centuries. In the seventeenth century, it was home to the respectable privateer Captain Kidd before he set sail into his infamous life of pirating. In the eighteenth century, it was home to banker Alexander Hamilton, who watched from his window the inauguration of George Washington at the site of the present Federal Hall National Memorial. It was also in the eighteenth century that merchants and bankers gathered under a buttonwood tree on Wall Street and established the New York Stock Exchange.

FRAUNCES TAVERN

Fraunces Tavern played a prominent role as a meeting place for revolutionaries during the eighteenth century and was the site for George Washington's famous farewell address to

his troops upon recapturing the city from the British. For many years the tavern served a dish reportedly created for the general, whose poor dental situation is well known. "Baked Chicken a la George Washington," was a casserole made of creamed chicken with rice and mushrooms—all soft ingredients for those with delicate mouths. The tavern is now a museum.

FRAUNCES TAVERN, N.Y. CITY.

COPYRIGHT 1906 BY GEO. P. HALL & SON, N.Y.

SINGER BUILDING AT NIGHT

Postcard artists used creative embellishments to add ambience to their cards. In both of these night views, buildings around the featured one were removed, adding to the perception of height and grandeur. The addition of clouds and moon creates a quiet, serene mood; however, the streets teeming with pedestrians reminds the viewer that this is still the city. The Singer Building, named for the Singer Sewing Machine Company that owned it, had its beginnings as a ten-story building completed in 1899. The addition of the architect Ernest T. Flagg's "tower" in 1908 brought its height to forty-seven stories, the tallest in the world until the Met Life Building on Madison Square was completed a year later.

CITY INVESTING BUILDING, BROADWAY & CORTLANDT ST.

The City Investing Building (1907) was an early example of the stepped-back design that became standard as taller buildings were being erected on small plots of land. This design was important in construction of these lofty buildings at the time because, in the days before fluorescent lighting, it allowed more natural light to get into the surrounding buildings. At thirty-four stories, the City Investing Building survived until 1968 when it was demolished to make way for the 1 Liberty Plaza Building.

CITY HALL PARK AND MUNICIPAL BUILDINGS, NEW YORK CITY.

CITY HALL PARK, MUNICIPAL BUILDING, NEWSPAPER ROW

In close proximity to both the financial district to the south and the legislative and judicial districts to the north, Park Row was an ideal location for New York's newspaper industry to flourish. It became known as Newspaper Row, and, at the turn of the last century, was home to nearly fifteen papers, including those whose buildings are visible in this postcard (left to right): the gold-domed New York World Building, the Sun Building, the Tribune Building, the Times Building, and the Potter Building, where *The Press* was published.

CITY PRISON (THE TOMBS)

The City Prison on Centre Street, nicknamed The Tombs for the type of Egyptian edifice the original building was reminiscent of, was notorious for some of the worst incarceration conditions in the country. This imposing Gothic structure, the second prison erected at this site, opened in 1902 and contained 320 cells and two chapels. Prisoners were led to trial at the Criminal Courts Building next door through the mid-air Bridge of Sighs connecting the two buildings. This structure was replaced in 1939 with the present city prison located across the street.

CITY PRISON, (THE TOMBS), NEW YORK CITY.

LOWER EAST SIDE

The waves of immigrants flooding the Lower East Side in the latter part of the
nineteenth century brought with them their cultures, ideologies, and traditions.
In this densely packed ethnically diverse area lived intellectuals, artists, and radicals.
Some of the best-known people of the twentieth century emerged throughout the
generations, including the composers George and Ira Gershwin and Irving Berlin,
the comedians Jimmy Durante and the Marx Brothers, and the politician Al Smith.

MONDAY MORNING ON THE EAST SIDE,
NEW YORK.

YAT BUN SING RESTAURANT

The first permanent resident of Chinese descent settled in the city 1825 and called himself William Brown. As the Chinese population grew, shops featuring exotic imported products and restaurants opened along Mott Street, in the heart of what became the Chinatown district. Li Hung Chang, a Chinese diplomat, is credited with exposing the American public to its first widely popular Asian-style dish that he called chop suey—a mixture of chopped vegetables, bean sprouts, celery, Chinese greens, and a little meat—which he made while visiting here in 1896. Chop suey restaurants like Yat Bun Sing opened up a whole new cuisine to Americans.

MULBERRY BEND PARK

Mulberry Bend, along Mulberry Street near Park and Bayard Streets, was known for some of the worst living conditions on the Lower East Side. Newspaper reporter Jacob Riis claimed the area was the most dangerous place in the city and worked with his camera to expose the public to how this "other half" lived. Due to his efforts, among other reformers, the worst of these tenements in the Bend were torn down in the 1890s and replaced with the Mulberry Bend Park in 1894. The name was changed to Columbus Park in 1911.

SAMMY'S ORIGINAL BOWERY GAY 90S

Sammy's Original Bowery Cabaret was founded by Sammy Fuchs (named honorary "Mayor of the Bowery" by Mayor William O'Dwyer in 1946), who aided the needy and homeless inhabitants of the Bowery and celebrated the glory days of vaudeville in his establishment. Above the bar, murals depicting such skid-row regulars as Boulevard Rose, Greenpoint Gertie, and Toothless Kate decorated the cabaret, and Sammy's revue featured a sentimental journey performed by aging vaudeville greats who were past their prime as performers but still a gang of fun.

WILLIAMSBURG BRIDGE APPROACH

Linking Manhattan and Brooklyn, the Williamsburg Bridge opened on December 21, 1903. The first person to cross it was Wally Owen in his fifty-six horsepower Speedster. Wally's round-trip was clocked at six minutes and fifty seconds; several policemen wandering about on the bridge barely escaped injury. The bridge was dubbed the Jews' Highway by the press because it opened rural Williamsburg to floods of Jewish immigrants from the crowded Lower East Side.

Williamsburg Bridge Approach, New York.

MANHATTAN BRIDGE APPROACH

The Manhattan Bridge was completed in 1909 during a six-year post-Consolidation building boom. The decorative grand plaza and colonnade installed in 1916 at the Manhattan entrance, inspired by the Prote St. Denis in Paris, has been chipped away at by city administrations and the elements and was almost torn down completely by an over-exuberant Robert Moses during bridge reconstruction in 1961. Though it never achieved the elegance depicted in this postcard, the colonnade, much to the annoyance of motorists today, is still a part of the bridge.

66:—Manhattan Bridge Approach, New York.

I am seeing Great Things

For many years after it was completed in 1902, the Flatiron Building was the tallest building in the Madison Square area. From the top of the twenty-one-story structure one could see Coney Island and the New Jersey Palisades. The north corner of the building at the six-foot-wide apex is one of the windiest spots in the city, and urban legend prevails that the phrase "23-skidoo" originated here. According to lore, young men used to gather at this area near 23rd Street, Fifth Avenue, and Broadway to watch the women's skirts blow as they walked by and police would use the phrase to move them along.

Metropolitan Life Insurance Co.'s Home Office Bldg., N. Y. City. Card cabinets for Ordinary Department, containing the records of more than $550,000,000 of Ordinary insurance.

Metropolitan Life Insurance Company

In the early part of the twentieth century, middle-class women in need of employment, such as those depicted in this card, could often find clerical positions in office environments. Lower-class immigrant women, however, were more likely to work in sweatshops or do piecework at home. Met Life, one of the largest insurers in the country, was an innovator in record-keeping technologies and was the first to use fledgling computer systems to process their data in the 1950s.

Madison Square Garden, New York.

Madison Square Garden

Standing on the site that once held the Union Depot of the New York and Harlem Railroad and another theater called Gilmore Gardens, Madison Square Garden, with a tower at 341 feet high, was the second-tallest building in New York City when it was completed in 1890. The tower was the scene of one of the most infamous murders in New York City: Stanford White, its architect, was shot there by Harry K. Thaw, the husband of actress Evelyn Nesbit, who was White's former lover.

I am seeing great things.—

Flatiron
Chelsea,
Greenwich
Village

ARABIAN NIGHTS BALL AND TURKEY TROT CONTEST

At this location for over thirty-five years, Madison Square Garden was used for various forms of entertainment, including exotic and outlandish events like the Arabian Nights Ball and Turkey Trot Contest. Other notables were the first national automobile show in 1900 and the wake of John Barleycorn in 1920 at the onset of prohibition. The last great event held there was the 1924 Democratic National Convention, where John W. Davis beat out New York's own Al Smith to win the nomination. In 1925 the Garden was razed to build the New York Life Insurance Company Building.

THE SIEGEL-COOPER DEPARTMENT STORE

Known as the Big Store, the Siegel-Cooper Department Store had seven floors and over fifteen acres of space to display merchandise. The store's "meet me at the fountain" slogan referred to the famed fountain that featured an eighteen-foot-high marble female figure by sculptor Daniel Chester French. The company declared bankruptcy in 1915 and the fountain was removed in 1918 when the department store was converted to a military hospital. The statue was ultimately sold to Forest Lawn Memorial Park in California in 1948. The building is still standing and is currently occupied by Bed, Bath & Beyond and T.J. Maxx.

The Siegel-Cooper Department Store, New York.

Union Square showing Battleship "Recruit," New York City.

UNION SQUARE SHOWING THE BATTLESHIP RECRUIT

Called Union Place in 1811 because it unites Broadway and 4th Avenue, Union Square has been used as a gathering place for George Washington's troops before taking official possession of New York from the British in 1783, rallies and labor protesters in the 1940s, and the final stop for the first Labor Day Parade. The mock battleship featured in this card was built in 1917 of wood and tin to encourage recruitment in the marines and the navy. Modeled after the *USS Maine,* 25,000 persons had enlisted here by the time it was dismantled in 1920.

WASHINGTON ARCH AND FOUNTAIN

In celebration of the centennial of George Washington's inauguration in 1889, a temporary wood and plaster arch was erected at Washington Square, and three years later it was replaced by the present seventy-seven-foot marble structure. In 1916 another celebration of sorts was held: a group of artists led by John Sloan and Marcel Duchamp forced open the door to the stairs leading to the top of the arch and held a midwinter party to declare the secession of Greenwich Village from the United States of America. They lit Japanese lanterns, read poems, fired cap pistols, and proclaimed the independence of the state of New Bohemia.

190:—WASHINGTON ARCH AND FOUNTAIN, NEW YORK CITY.

44258

Hotel Chelsea,
West Twenty-third Street
at Seventh Avenue,
New York City.

HOTEL CHELSEA AT 222 WEST 23RD ST.

The eleven-story Hotel Chelsea opened in 1884 as one of the first cooperative apartment buildings in New York City. A list of some of the famous people who have lived there reads like a who's who of the art, theater, and literary circles: Sarah Bernhardt, Lillian Russell, Mark Twain, O'Henry, Thomas Wolfe, John Sloan, Arthur Miller (after his break up with Marilyn Monroe), Tennessee Williams, and Jackson Pollock. The survivors of the *Titanic* stayed here for a few days, and Dylan Thomas collapsed here after the alcoholic binge from which he ultimately died.

Pennsylvania R. R. Station, New York.

PENNSYLVANIA RR STATION

Inspired by classic designs, Pennsylvania Station, Charles McKim's crowning achievement, opened in 1910. Its proportions were staggering: the marble-columned waiting room, at 150 feet high, 300 feet long and 110 feet wide, was large enough to contain a fifteen-story skyscraper. The glass and steel train concourse, at 340 feet long and 210 feet wide, could almost contain a football field. Despite this grandeur, with the decline in rail use, the station fell into disrepair and was demolished in 1963. This tragedy prompted the establishment of the Landmarks Preservation Commission.

Hotel Pennsylvania, New York City.

HOTEL PENNSYLVANIA

In the days before telephone dials were common, exchanges with names such as "Butterfield" and "Pennsylvania" were developed to denote geographic areas, much like area codes today. The Pennsylvania Hotel and its exchange were made famous at the time of this convention by Glen Miller's 1940s song "Pennsylvania 6-5000," the telephone number to dial to make a reservation at the hotel's Cafe Rouge, where the band often played. By the 1950s the phone company decided these alphanumeric exchanges were both difficult to remember and confusing they were eventually phased out in the 1960s.

R. H. MACY COMPANY

R. H. Macy, a whaling captain turned merchant, whose red star tattoo became the symbol for the store, opened the first Macy's in 1858 at 14th Street in the shopping district known as Ladies Mile. By the time of Macy's death in 1877, he had established many of the retail techniques the store would be most famous for: cash-only transactions, vigorous advertising, a money-back guarantee, clearance sales, fixed prices, and attractive window displays for each season. In 1888 Isador and Nathan Strauss took over operations of the store and expanded its operations by moving it to the current location on Herald Square in 1902.

GIMBEL BROTHERS BUILDING

When Gimbel Brothers opened in 1910 one block from R. H. Macy's, it created stiff competition. Its 390 departments, if lined up next to each other as individual specialty shops, would have stretched forty blocks and visually made the store's motto "You can buy anything at Gimbel's" ring true. Aside from the usual store goods, one could purchase theater tickets, send telegrams, complete banking transactions, and it offered such amenities as a beauty salon and an art gallery. It was in this gallery that the paintings of Anna Mary Robertson ("Grandma") Moses were first exhibited around Thanksgiving 1940. The building was reconfigured in the late 1980s and is now the Manhattan Mall.

Detail:
R.H. Macy Company,
New York, NY

MACY·S
IT'S
SMART
TO BE
THRIFTY

TIMES SQUARE & SPECTACULARS

When New York's first subway line opened in 1904, New York Times publisher Aldoph Ochs moved his newspaper from Newspaper Row downtown up to the intersection of 42nd Street and Broadway. He persuaded city administrators to call the subway stop The Times, and the word square soon followed. A later visitor to Times Square described her experiences there:

"October 20, 1949.

Dear Ruth, Betty and I finally made it. Flew over on Sunday and the trip was grand. We have seen so many things and tonight we have standing room only to see 'South Pacific.' On our way from 'Lend an Ear' this afternoon saw Jack Dempsey in front of the Astor, also Rosalind Russell last nite in a radio broadcast. (signed) Evelyn."

PUB. BY I. H. BLANCHARD CO. N.Y.

1040.   Times Building, New York.

A HAPPY NEW YEAR, 1904

The year the New York Times moved uptown, it celebrated New Year's Eve with an elaborate fireworks display. Drawing some of the crowd who usually gathered in front of Trinity Church to ring in the New Year, it was a decided success and thus a tradition was born. Due to safety concerns with exploding fireworks over such a large crowd, the company instituted the lighted ball drop instead in 1907. Every year since then, this ball has descended into the New Year with the exception of 1943 and 1944, during the blackout periods of World War II.

TIMES SQUARE

Times Square was christened the Great White Way when flashing electric lights were added to the Times building shortly after it opened. On September 22, 1906, the Tribune declared, "New York is the electric city . . . this glittering trail along Broadway." Very visible in the middle of this 1920s view of Times Square is the triangular concrete island that separates Broadway and Seventh Avenue, which was a hangout in the teens and twenties for out-of-work vaudevillians, who referred to it as the beach.

Times Square, New York.

This spectacular sign over the PLANTERS PEANUT
York City, contains 15,000 brilliantly lighted bulbs
20 feet high, who magically brings various Planters
The Giant "PLANTERS PEANUTS" in neon flashes
and famous "PLANTERS PEANUTS" flow from
the 5¢ bag at bottom of sign.

1560 Broadway

STORE on Broadway, New
d an animated Mr. Peanut,
roducts into the magic ball.
n and off

MR. PEANUT

THE PEANUT STORE
1560 BROADWAY

"Mr. Peanut" was based
on a design by a four-
teen-year-old Virginian
who submitted his
drawing of a peanut
with arms and legs in a
competition for the
company in 1916. With
the additions of the
monocle, cane, and top
hat by the company,
the character was born.
The store at 1560
Broadway sold freshly
roasted peanuts, and
many days a male
employee dressed as
Mr. Peanut could be
seen parading outside
the shop, greeting
people and dispensing
free samples to entice
shoppers. The store
closed in the 1960s.

7B-H476

THE INDIAN GRILL ROOM, HOTEL ASTOR

THE INDIAN GRILL ROOM, HOTEL ASTOR, NEW YORK

The eleven-story Hotel Astor opened in 1904, just as the area was becoming fashionable. The first air-conditioned hotel in the northeast, it was a popular destination for the theater crowd, maintaining a roof garden and dining rooms, such as the Indian Grill Room, which was decorated with priceless artifacts and museum-quality pieces. The building survived into the 1960s but was demolished in 1968 to make way for an office building. This grand dame did not go easily, however. According to accounts from the wrecking crew, she was "built like a fortress" and even as huge wrecking balls smashed into her outer walls, sometimes only chips of brick and dust were removed.

INTERNATIONAL CASINO & WRIGLEY'S SIGN

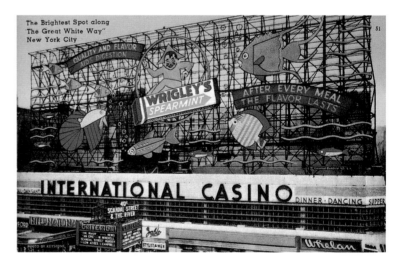

Spectacular animated signs give Times Square its razzle-dazzle. At night they literally turn on the entire area. The first signs used plain white light bulbs, but the introduction of neon in 1927 opened up a rainbow of possibilities. The Wrigley's sign, one of the most famous, was designed by O. J. Gude, who is credited as being "the father of the Great White Way" for all of his lighted-sign innovations. This display contained seventy miles of insulated wire, had 209,608 lamp receptacles, and boasted 1,084 feet of neon tubing.

TIMES SQUARE AT NIGHT (KLEENEX SIGN)

The fanciful Kleenex sign, moved to various locations in the square, featured the cartoon character Little Lulu. It consisted of thirty-two different Lulus who skipped across the sign illuminating the sixteen-foot letters spelling out Kleenex as she passed. When she reached the last letter, she jumped down on a sheet of Kleenex in its box and then slid down the fifty-foot box. A giant hand would then grab the tissue and pull it, demonstrating the pop-up nature of the packaging. The 25,000 feet of various-colored neon tubing allowed this show to be repeated in five different colors.

BOND SPECTACULAR WATERFALL SIGN IN TIMES SQUARE

The Bond sign atop the Bond Clothing Store was one of the most elaborate spectaculars to grace Times Square. It used 21,500 electric lightbulbs and enough colored neon tubing to stretch over forty blocks. The waterfall was 27 feet high and 132 feet long and employed twenty-three giant pumps to keep the 10,000 gallons flowing continuously over the falls. The delicately clothed giant statues, weighing over twelve tons combined, were more than five stories high. Designed by Douglas Leigh in 1948, it was replaced in 1954 by another of his creations, for Pepsi-Cola, which can be seen in the distance in the Kleenex postcard below.

WALDORF-ASTORIA HOTEL

Considered one of the most elegant hotels of its day, the Waldorf-Astoria was the end result of a familial squabble between two of the Astor clan whose gracious mansions lined this portion of Fifth Avenue in the nineteenth century. William Waldorf Astor, who supposedly loathed his aunt Caroline Schermerhorn Astor, decided to erect a thirteen-story hotel next to her mansion. Annoyed by this intrusion, Caroline took her revenge by building a larger seventeen-story structure next door. The Waldorf, completed in 1893 and noted for being the first hotel to offer breakfast in bed, allow smoking in mixed company, and let unescorted women enter through the lobby; and the Astoria completed in 1897 and known as the first hotel with a roof garden, where ice-skating was offered in winter were eventually joined by a corridor; and they both flourished. The grandeur was short-lived, however. In 1929 both buildings were demolished to make way for the Empire State Building, and the remains were unceremoniously dumped offshore in the Atlantic.

Waldorf-Astoria Hotel, New York City.

LONDON DOG AND BIRD SHOP.

THREE HUNDRED FIFTH AVENUE, CORNER 31ST STREET, NEW YORK.

LONDON DOG AND BIRD SHOP

The London Dog and Bird Shop was one type of specialty shop that made Fifth Avenue a famous shopping district. This advertising card has a hand-written message on the back that reads, "Dear Madame: We are offering a holiday special & wish to give our customers the benefit of same—a cage & stand (any color) with a canary free at $10.00. If interested kindly let us hear. London Bird and Dog Shop. (signed) Mrs. Zimmerman"

Fifth Avenue Looking North From 42nd St.

In 1922, seven traffic towers such as this, designed by architect Joseph H. Freedlander, were erected along Fifth Avenue between Washington Square and 59th Street in an attempt to control the increased motor traffic. These twenty-three-foot structures had bronze and glass cages, heated by an electric stove and manned by police officers who controlled the traffic with red, amber, and green lights. Determined to be more obstructive to motorists than helpful, these structures were removed in 1929, five years after the automatic traffic lights suspended along Broadway proved to be more successful.

FIFTH AVENUE LOOKING NORTH FROM 42ND ST., NEW YORK.

Double Deck Bus on Fifth Avenue

The Fifth Avenue Coach Company began operating horse-drawn buses in 1885, and by 1905 they had switched to motorized double-decker buses. At the time this card was produced, these buses ran from Washington Square north along Fifth Avenue to 90th Street; the fare was ten cents. This open-topped model was discontinued in 1946 and the closed-top models ended service in 1953. Note the traffic going in both directions on this card. Fifth Avenue was one of the last of the avenues in Manhattan to be converted to one-way traffic, for safety reasons, in 1966.

DOUBLE DECK BUS, ON FIFTH AVENUE, NEW YORK CITY.

ROCKEFELLER CENTER

Sitting on one million square feet (twenty-two acres) of prime Manhattan real estate, this "example of urban planning for the future" has been a city icon since its early days. From its underground network of shops, boutiques, and restaurants, officially called the Underground Concourse but referred to by those who frequent it as the Catacombs, to its elaborate rooftop gardens, Rockefeller Center functions as both an international center of business and an entertainment destination. Rockefeller Center's seven roof gardens were designed to add greenery to the window views of the center's buildings. They were: the International Gardens (on the four six-story buildings lining Fifth Avenue), the Garden of Nations (on the eleventh-story setback of the RCA Building), and two atop Radio City Music Hall and the Central Theater (now gone). Tours were available until the late 1960s.

156:—ROCKEFELLER CENTER BY NIGHT, NEW YORK CITY.

OBSERVATION ROOF, RO

ROCKEFELLER CENTER BY NIGHT

In this night view of Rockefeller Center from Sixth Avenue, the RCA Building (now the GE Building) at 30 Rockefeller Center stands in sharp contrast to the four-story row houses that made up the neighborhood before construction began on the center in the 1930s. The 6th Avenue el, also visible here, became obsolete in the 1940s when the IND subway line was constructed underneath the avenue.

ENGLISH GARDEN, GARDEN OF THE NATIONS, ROCKEFELLER CENTER

The English Garden was one of twelve including the French, Dutch, and Spanish among others that made up the Garden of Nations on the eleventh-floor setback of the RCA Building, directly over the NBC studios. Built in 1934, these formal gardens contained rocks, statuary and horticultural specimens from the countries they represented. Until it was deemed unprofitable in 1938, tours were conducted and hostesses, dressed in the clothing of the countries they represented, were on hand to greet visitors.

ENGLISH GARDEN, GARDENS OF THE NATIONS, ROCKEFELLER CENTER, NEW YORK CITY   67

JAPANESE GARDEN AT NIGHT, ROCKEFELLER CENTER

The gardens were lit at night, and the back of this card describes in detail the splendor of the Japanese Garden in the Garden of Nations at that time: "Around an illuminated snowscene lanterns are grouped three lead cranes, symbolic of the past, present, and future. In the foreground a shallow stream winds under an arched bridge overhung by a weeping cherry tree. In the background against the walls of a Japanese tea house can be seen flowering azaleas and rhododendrons."

156   Japanese Garden at Night, Rockefeller Center, New York City

...LER CENTER. NEW YORK.

42270

OBSERVATION ROOF, ROCKEFELLER CENTER

As a means to bring revenue to Rockefeller Center, an observation deck was part of the design for the 850-foot RCA Building. Located on the 70th floor, this 200-foot-long and 20-foot-wide platform offered breathtaking views of the city, the rivers, and New Jersey beyond, as visible in this card. The observatory was entered through a small elevator outside the Rainbow Room, but access to it was closed when the Rainbow Room was renovated in 1986.

Pershing Square Hotels,
John Mc E. Bowman, President,
New York City.

The New Murray Hill. The Belmont. The Biltmore. Hotel Commodore.

PERSHING SQUARE HOTELS, NEW MURRAY HILL, THE BELMONT, THE BILTMORE, HOTEL COMMODORE

Pershing Square, at Park Avenue and 42nd Street, was created on the site of the old Grand Union Hotel when it was demolished in 1914. This modest park survived for almost ten years until the Pershing Square Building was erected there. The hotels in this Grand Central District were constructed as part of a plan to provide accommodations for travelers using the terminal. The Murray Hill and the Belmont were demolished, the Hotel Commodore was renovated and is now the Grand Hyatt, and the Biltmore was remodeled and now contains the Bank of America offices.

RESTAURANT WAITERS, THE BILTMORE

The Biltmore's Palm Court, with its famed clock, was the gathering place for hotel visitors and college students alike. The elegant Bowman Room offered dining a la carte. Considered expensive for the day, the 1930s prices included: Blue Point oysters at fifty cents (cocktail sauce an additional ten cents), breast of duck Singapore for $1.75, and sirloin steak for two at $4.50. The Men's Bar was a place where men could enjoy their drinking without the distraction of the fairer sex. If a woman did venture in, the patrons would aggressively applaud until she left or was escorted out. By the late 1960s, women were admitted, but the bar closed shortly after the male-only tradition ended.

RESTAURANT WAITERS, THE BILTMORE, NEW YORK

MAIN CONCOURSE, GRAND CENTRAL TERMINAL

Above the bustle and chaos of the Grand Central's main concourse is the 125-foot vaulted ceiling with its painted serene blue canopy and 2,500 stars making up the constellations of the zodiac. Many passersby marvel at the beauty of this but few recognize that, with the exception of Orion the Hunter, these shapes are depicted in reverse. One probable reason for the artist Paul Helleu's design is that he was inspired by medieval illuminated manuscripts, which often depicted the cosmos as seen from an observer outside the universe. Recently stripped of more than seventy-five years of grime, this ceiling has been restored to the beautiful condition as at the time of this card.

GRAND CENTRAL, KODAK DISPLAY

Fondly remembered by many of the 650,000 persons who daily travel through Grand Central, the Kodak Colorama display was installed in 1950. For almost fifty years the 18-foot-high, 60-foot-wide colorful transparencies graced the spacious main terminal concourse, and by them, viewers were able to track the changing styles and seasons. In the late 1980s, this display was one of the first add-ons to come down during renovations.

14825

PARK AVENUE LOOKING NORTH FROM 46TH STREET

Park Avenue, with its green center islands that inspired the name, has been synonymous with elegance and class for over 100 years. In the early part of the twentieth century, it was known for its gracious residential living in the stately brick and terra-cotta apartment buildings that lined the avenue. During the prosperous post-World War II era, however, these properties became too valuable to continue as residential and were torn down to build the glass-and-steel office buildings such as the Seagram and Lever Buildings the area is known for today.

PARK AVENUE SOUTH

Towering above the Grand Central Terminal, the thirty-four-story New York Central Building, headquarters of the railroad at that time, was built in 1929. Planted right in the middle of Park Avenue, this building's characteristic cupola-topped pyramidal roof graced

the view up the avenue for thirty-three years until the fifty-nine-story concrete-and-glass Pan Am Building (now the Met Life Building), placed between the New York Central Building and Grand Central Terminal in 1963, spoiled the view. The decorations of the 1920s-era cars and a policeman enhance the fun mood of this card.

QUEENSBORO BRIDGE
AND
BLACKWELL'S ISLAND

The proximity to, but isolation from, Manhattan made the two-mile Blackwell's Island (later Welfare Island, 1921, and currently Roosevelt Island, 1971) an ideal location for public buildings to detain the city's least desirables. The city penitentiary, built in the 1830s, held such infamous incarcerates as the corrupt politician "Boss" Tweed and the scandalous Mae West. America's first insane asylum, built in

Queensboro Bridge and Blackwell's Island, New York City

1829 on the island, was a popular tourist stop, and visitors included Charles Dickens. Visible in this card are the tenements and stockyards along the river, which were replaced by the UN complex in the late 1940s.

BELLEVUE HOSPITAL

Bellevue Hospital, depicted here in the clouds, is actually located between First Avenue, and the East River, and 26th and 29th Streets. It opened in 1826 and since then has expanded numerous times (from 550 beds in the 1850s to 2,700 beds in the 1950s) and has been the location of many firsts at U.S. hospitals: the first to use hypodermic syringes (1856), the first to provide a hospital ambulance (1869), and the first to perform a cesarean section (1887).

New Bellevue Hospital, New York City.

CENTRAL PARK

"About one o'clock the shoppers from Bergdorf-Goodman's and the smart little shops of the neighboring side streets forgather here to meet husbands summoned up from downtown to discuss the latest trends in hats. By four, the scene has changed; now it is the younger set, the debs and sub-debs of the season, with their escorts, who sit in the lounge or at tables by the windows over tea, highballs, or old fashioneds. On Saturdays there is tea dancing. By seven, evening clothes are in the ascendancy, although not de rigueur at the dinner hour; later in the evening you must dress if you would dance. Meanwhile, entertainment, usually by a dancing team and usually excellent and very, very popular, is provided" (Middleton, Scudder. *Dining, Wining and Dancing in New York*).

The Plaza, 5th Ave. at Central Park, New York City.

THE PLAZA, 5TH AVE. AT CENTRAL PARK

The elegant Plaza hotel opened to great fanfare on October 1, 1907, and the event was attended by the Vanderbilts (whose mansions had lined that area at one time), the actress Lillian Russell, and businessman "Diamond Jim" Brady (known as the first person to own an automobile in New York City). This postcard, with its view of the vast terrain of Central Park and the horizon in the distance, gives the impression that the hotel is in the bucolic countryside rather than the middle of the city.

THE MALL, CENTRAL PARK

In an effort to give New York City some of the refinement of European cities, the wealthier merchants and landowners of the 1850s proposed this landscaped public park for the city so that the upper classes would have a place to ride in their carriages and the lower classes would have a healthy alternative to the pubs. Upon its completion, the Mall, also known as the Literary Walk because of the statues of famous writers residing there, quickly became an elegant promenade for those who preferred to go on foot.

The Mall, Central Park, New York.

GONDOLAS IN CENTRAL PARK,

The first boats on the lake appeared in 1860; soon swan boats, rowboats, canoes, gondolas, and canopy-covered dories were available for pleasure seekers. An omnibus boat, that started at Bethesda Terrace, picked up passengers at six points along the shoreline, and other boats were available for hire by the hour. The first Venetian gondola was presented by Park Commissioner John A. C. Gray in 1862. These boats were in use at the lake into the 1900s.

Gondolas in Central Park, New York.

DONKEYS IN CENTRAL PARK

After 1874, for ten cents, children could ride along the Mall in carts drawn by a team of goats or ride on a donkey from Bow Bridge up to Vista Rock and back. By the next year, pony rides were also offered for ten cents. This card is postmarked 1909 and the back is inscribed, "Dear Little Russell—How would you like to ride on one of these donkeys. Be a good boy and help Dan Dan and Aunt Stella With love and kisses, Mama"

n Central Park, New York.

47

VINE ARCH BRIDGE

The Gapstow Bridge, or Vine Arch Bridge, built of Manhattan schist and spanning the waters of the pond at the southeast corner of the park, is one of the numerous uniquely designed bridges in Central Park. The first swans that resided in the pond were a gift from the City of Hamburg in 1860. Nine out of the twelve originals died but were replaced by others by the Royal Companies of Vintners and Dyers of London. The vines and the swans are gone from this view today.

180:—VINE ARCH BRIDGE. CENTRAL PARK, NEW YORK.

40780

Columbus Circle, N. Y.

THE WEST SIDE

COLUMBUS CIRCLE

In October 1892 the Italian government dedicated this granite monument depicting the *Nina*, *Pinta*, and *Santa Maria* to the people of America. The statue of Columbus that now graces the top of it was placed there two years later. The Tichenor Riding School, prominent in this card, was one of the many Upper West Side riding stables whose close proximity to Central Park made the location ideal for horseback riding. The building was razed in the late 1960s to make way for the Gulf and Western Plaza at 1 Central Park West. This was later converted to the present Trump International Hotel.

The Autopiano factories in New York City, (50th to 52nd Sts., facing the Hudson River) the largest factories in the world devoted to the Manufacture of Player Pianos exclusively.

The Atlantic Battleship Fleet passing the Autopiano Factories.

48

THE AUTOPIANO FACTORY IN NEW YORK CITY — THE ATLANTIC BATTLESHIP FLEET PASSING THE AUTOPIANO FACTORIES

Advertised as the choice of the U.S. Navy, the autopianos built in these factories around 50th Street along the Hudson River were used aboard ships, like the ones passing in review here, dating from around World War I. The back of the card explains that "the remarkable manner in which the autopiano stands up under hard usage and all sorts of climatic changes on these warships is proof of its durability." As strong as these pianos were purported to be, the popularity of radio and phonographs led to their decline by the 1940s.

COLUMBIAN UNIVERSITY

Once called Asylum Hill for the Bloomingdale Insane Asylum, that operated at this location until 1895, Broadway at 116th Street is now home to Columbia University. The subway station depicted here is one of three that graced Broadway from 72nd to 116th Streets and were designed by Heins & La Farge, creators of the Cathedral of St. John the Divine. During renovations that moved the subway entrances to either side of Broadway, this station and the one at 103rd Street were removed. The one on the triangle at Broadway at 72nd Street remains.

Columbian University, New York City.

CHARLES SCHWAB'S RESIDENCE

Completed in 1906, this French chateau style mansion at Riverside Drive and 73rd Street, containing seventy-five rooms, two elevators, a chapel and the largest pipe organ in a private New York residence, was built at a cost of $3 million, with an additional $5 million spent for other interior furnishings. Schwab, who made his millions in the steel industry, lived there until 1939 when he and his wife passed away. Known as one of the most beautiful mansions in the world, it was razed in 1948 to make way for an apartment building.

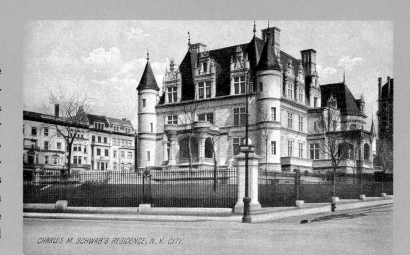

CHARLES M. SCHWAB'S RESIDENCE, N. Y. CITY.

180:—TRAFFIC ON WEST SIDE HIGHWAY, LOOKING NORTH FROM 46TH STREET, NEW YORK CITY.

44248

TRAFFIC ON WEST SIDE HIGHWAY, LOOKING NORTH FROM 46TH STREET

Under construction between 1931 and 1948, this elevated structure ran from Rector Street to 72nd Street and was created to alleviate some of the traffic congestion on the city's west side. This roadway was successful for a while, providing both a quick means of getting from one end of the island to the other and scenic views of New Jersey and the ocean liners docked along the Hudson. But as the decades progressed, the highway was in a constant state of disrepair, and most of it was eventually demolished.

49

CLAREMONT INN AND GARDENS

This outdoor dining area and dance floor was part of the Claremont, a charming country inn at Riverside Drive and 124th Street. Built around the turn of the nineteenth century, it was owned as a private residence by Michael Hogan, friend to Prince William and Joseph Bonaparte, Napoleon's brother. From 1860 until it closed in 1948, it was a popular restaurant destination for New Yorkers seeking a close-by retreat from the bustle of the city. Diners could enjoy rare seafood, such as roe from shad caught in the Claremont's very own nets in the Hudson River opposite the inn in the grand dining room or dance to a live band under the stars on this outdoor garden terrace.

HARLEM

The Harlem night scene had its start during the days of Prohibition. Night clubs and speakeasies such as the Cotton Club, the Plantation, Connie's Inn, and Small's Paradise, many of which only allowed white clientele, catered to the downtown crowd who enjoyed the raucous atmosphere these places provided. The Cotton Club, open from 1922 to 1937 at 142nd Street and Lenox Avenue, a place frequented by Mayor Jimmie Walker, featured such entertainers as Duke Ellington, Cab Calloway, Ethel Waters, Josephine Baker, and a young Lena Horne before these jazz performers were accepted downtown. Other places such as the Apollo (1914) on 125th Street featured variety shows with such rising stars as Sarah Vaughan, and the Audubon Theater (1912) on Broadway and 165th Street had movies as well as dancing.

SAVOY BALLROOM

Known as the "showplace of Harlem," the Savoy Ballroom at Lenox Avenue and 140th Street opened March 12, 1926, and during its thirty-two years, many went "stompin' at the savoy." The management sponsored "band battles" between such notables as Louis Armstrong, Mildred Bailey, Count Basie, Ella Fitzgerald, Lionel Hampton and Gene Krupa, and dance contests that inspired such famous dances as the "Mutiny Swing," the "Suzy-Q," the "Big Aoole," the "Shag" and the "Lindy-Hop."

SAVOY BALLROOM —— Lenox Avenue and 140th Street —— NEW YORK

The Last Harlem Goat.

THE LAST HARLEM GOAT

Though not as well known on the tourist circuit as its close neighbor Grant's Tomb, the Last Harlem Goat was a stuffed nanny who graced the display window of Friedgen's Drugstore at Amsterdam Avenue and 118th Street. This early example of a divided-back advertising card was published by Charles Friedgen, owner of the drugstore, and printed in Germany, most likely when that country dominated the postcard printing business before World War I.

ALHAMBRA THEATRE

Vaudeville, the essential New York form of entertainment combining singing, dance, comedy, and acrobatics was created to reach a wider audience than traditional forms of theatrical entertainment. The Lower East Side was its birthplace, and as interest in it grew, theaters outside of the area, in Times Square, Harlem and the other boroughs, flourished.

Located on the southwest corner of Seventh Avenue and 124th Street, the Alhambra opened on April 15, 1905, as a house for high-class vaudeville at the height of its popularity. It is known as one of the few theaters to offer subscriptions, but its stint was short-lived, closing with vaudeville's decline after the 1920s.

Seventh Avenue, North of One Hundred and Twenty-fifth Street, New York.

THE BRONX, BROOKLYN, QUEENS AND STATEN ISLAND, TOO

THE BRONX

POE COTTAGE, KINGSBRIDGE ROAD

Hoping that the salubrious country air might help to relieve his consumptive wife, Edgar Allen Poe moved from Manhattan to this $100-a-year farmhouse on Kingsbridge Road in 1846. She died shortly after, but he stayed on until 1849, writing such many notable poems as *Annabel Lee, The Bells,* and *Eureka.* As the area around the house was developed, large apartment buildings encroached on this bucolic setting, and in 1913 the house was moved by the city to a safer place across the street. In 1917 it became a museum dedicated to Poe.

NOAH'S ARK IN THE CHILDREN'S ZOO, NEW YORK ZOOLOGICAL PARK

Safari rides on exotic beasts such as llamas and camels, in addition to this whimsical Noah's Ark playground, were just a few of the wonders awaiting young ones at the Children's Zoo, which opened in 1941 and closed in 1980 for renovation. Contained in the New York Zoological Park in the Bronx, which opened in 1899, the zoo itself was innovative in its day, creating environments in which rare animals could be studied and bred. Now called the Bronx Zoo/Wildlife Conservation Park, it continues this work.

Noah's Ark in the Children's Zoo, New York Zoological Park

C. W. V.
Model Gift Home of 1952
Williamsbridge Road, corner Stell Pl.
Bronx, N. Y.
FREE — Public Inspection — FREE
Daily 2:00 to 10:30 P.M.
March 14th thru June 27th

C. W. V. Model Gift Home of 1952 Williamsbridge Road

The Catholic War Veterans raffled gift homes such as this in all the outer boroughs in post-War New York. The back of this card reads: *"Presenting the CWV Model Gift Home of 1952, Opened Daily March 14th thru June 27th. Valued at $40,000 completely furnished . . . with plot and free and clear of all encumbrances, this beautiful 7-room Model Home with finished basement and recreation room, includes a new 1952 Ford Automobile. All of this a Major Feature of the Bronx, Westchester, and New York County Chapters, Catholic War Veterans USA in connection with the Bronx Home Show of 1952 at the Hotel Concourse Plaza, Grand Concourse at East 161st Street, Bronx. . . ."*

The Center Park, Parkchester

Built between 1938 and 1942 on almost 130 acres, Parkchester was the first large-scale housing development in the Bronx that was not a city. However this massive, 171-building, 40,000-resident complex contained many city amenities, including a large parking garage, a movie theater, bowling alley, restaurants, and other shops. Historically significant as an innovative residential community, in the late 1960s portions of Parkchester were converted to co-ops, and it continues to be a popular, low-cost, convenient alternative to Manhattan.

The Center Park, Parkchester, The Bronx, New York, N. Y.   176

73414

BROOKLYN

Concord Baptist Church of Christ, Brooklyn, N. Y.

Dr. James B. Adams, Pastor

CONCORD BAPTIST CHURCH OF CHRIST
Founded in May 1847, Concord Baptist Church is one of the many houses of worship in the City of Churches. It was created by members of the Abyssinian Baptist Church who had difficulty attending the services in Manhattan due to a lack of dependable means of travel before the Brooklyn Bridge was constructed. The first pastor was the abolitionist Samson White, who was followed in 1850 by Leonard Black, a fugitive slave. The Reverend James B. Adams, pictured here, became pastor in 1920 and led the congregation until 1948. On October 2, 1952, the church burned, but it was rebuilt by 1956.

54

BROOKLYN PARAMOUNT BUILDING, BROOKLYN, N. Y.

BROOKLYN'S PARAMOUNT BUILDING
Billed as the first movie theater built for talkies, the Paramount on Flatbush and Dekalb Avenues opened in 1928 with the movie *Manhattan Cocktail*. Alan Freed, who coined the term "rock and roll" in 1951, staged revues here while working for the radio station WINS. By the early 1960s, due to pressures from Long Island University, which had purchased it a few years prior, the movie house showed its last feature, *Hatari*, with John Wayne, in August 1962. The next year it was converted to a gym, though its famous Wurlitzer organ still played on.

HOTEL ST. GEORGE SWIMMING POOL
Clark Street, Brooklyn, N. Y.

HOTEL ST. GEORGE SWIMMING POOL

Though modest when it opened in 1885, the St. George Hotel in Brooklyn Heights expanded several times and by 1930, contained 2,632 rooms, making it the largest hotel in New York City. The spectacular view of Manhattan from the roof restaurant and the indoor salt-water swimming pool (pictured here) were its most noted features. The 40 x 120 foot pool, built in the 1930s at a cost of $1.3 million, was used by such aquatic celebrities as Johnny Weissmuller, Buster Crabbe, and the synchronized swimmers featured at the 1939 New York World's Fair.

FLYING TURNS—CONEY ISLAND THRILLING RIDE. CONEY ISLAND. N. Y. 22

CONEY ISLAND'S "FLYING TURNS"

In 1884, the world's first roller coaster opened on West 10th Street in Coney Island. Called the Switchback Railway, it was 600 feet long, 50 feet high at its highest point, and was powered by gravity. By 1934, when the Flying Turns ride opened at Steeplechase, forty-four roller coasters had been introduced to Coney Island, including its most famous, the Cyclone (1927). Flying Turns, which employed a steep vertical drop and a series of figure eights, was enjoyed by thrill-seekers for five years until it was destroyed by fire in 1939.

56

LONG ISLAND INDIANS

Brooklyn's original inhabitants, the Canarsee Indians, dwelt in a number of settlements—in what is now the Navy Yard, in Flatlands, and in Gravesend. Perhaps the first group to utter the classic Brooklyn cry, "There goes the neighborhood!" when the Dutch arrived, the Canarsees began a westward trek that would take them as far as the Illinois country in about 1745. Later, European immigrants to the borough continued a tradition they brought from the Old World. On Thanksgiving, children dressed up as Indians or paupers and begged for food and trinkets, much like Halloween today.

QUEENS

LONG ISLAND'S FINEST RUG AND CARPET CENTER

Postmarked 1952, this card is an advertisement for the E. J. Clark Carpet Shop on Northern Boulevard in Flushing. The shop had a large selection of domestic and imported rugs and carpets and featured "tackless" installation. They also advertised such amenities as plenty of parking and, if a customer was not able to reach the store, they would send a representative with samples of their merchandise right to their door. Adding to the '50s feel of this card is a now-classic woodie station wagon that may have been used to deliver samples.

LONG ISLAND'S FINEST RUG AND CARPET CENTER

PLENTY OF PARKING SPACE   OPEN DAILY 9:00 A.M. TIL 9:00 P.M.

RUG CLEANING   CARPETS E. J CLARK RUGS

223-01 NORTHERN BLVD. AT CROSS ISLAND PARKWAY, BAYSIDE, N. Y.   •   Telephone: Bayside 9-4000

"Best Buy Mercury"

McGOLDRICK MERCURY

McGOLDRICK MERCURY MOTORS
415 WILLIS AVENUE, WILLISTON PARK, N. Y.
Pioneer 6-3700

McGOLDRICK MERCURY MOTORS

The planners of the 1939 New York World's Fair in Flushing encouraged the construction of parkways and traffic arteries in the vicinity of the fairgrounds to accommodate the large crowds attending the fair. This development opened up Queens to vehicular traffic as never before. Automobile dealerships such as McGoldrick Mercury Motors, along Willis Avenue, catered to the continued use of the car in Queens.

ROCKAWAY BEACH

Due to its great distance from the more populated areas of the city, Rockaway Beach was initially developed as an exclusive resort for the rich in the middle of the nineteenth century, because they were the ones who could afford to travel to this remote area. With the completion of the Brooklyn Bridge and the coming of the railroad in the 1870s, however, it became popular with the lower and middle classes. The Rockaway Beach Amusement Park opened in 1901, which led to a great expansion of the area for both weekend and summer vacationers.

ROCKAWAY BEACH, N. Y.

THOMPSON AVENUE VIADUCT, ASTORIA, L. I.

LOOSE-WILES, SUNSHINE BISCUITS, THOMPSON AVENUE VIADUCT, ASTORIA

Called the Thousand Window Bakery after it was built in 1914, the Loose-Wiles Sunshine Biscuit Company factory was the largest bakery in the world until 1955. Along with other factories, such as Adams Chewing Gum, Silver Cup, and Eveready, it made up a heavily industrial area of Long Island City, which fell into disuse after the 1950s. The Sunshine company moved to New Jersey in the 1960s, and this factory was renovated in the 1980s to become the International Design Center New York. The Silver Cup Bakery was converted to a movie studio in 1983.

STATEN ISLAND

Bathing Scene at Midland Beach N. Y.

BATHING SCENE AT MIDLAND BEACH

During the heyday of the seaside summer resorts at the turn of the last century, Midland Beach, on Staten Island's east shore, was one of the most popular. On hot summer days, excursion boats from Manhattan and New Jersey would arrive, dropping off thrill-seekers escaping the heat to enjoy the cool sea breezes, rides, and other amusements the boardwalk and beach had to offer. By the 1940s the area was in decline due to economic conditions, pollution and several fires. Though the romantic feeling of the beach is gone, Midland Beach is still used as a swimming and recreational area.

ST. GEORGE FERRY, STATEN ISLAND

Until the completion of the Outerbridge Crossing and the Goethals Bridge in 1928, the only way on and off Staten Island was by ferry. In the 1880s entrepreneur Erastus Wiman, credited for much of the transportation system on the island, moved the ferry terminal from Tompkinsville to St. George, a shorter trip from the other boroughs, and the St. George terminal area became the "gateway to Staten Island." The modest terminal pictured here was replaced by the current one in 1949.

St. George Ferry, Staten Island, N.Y.

TRIP THE LIGHT FANTASTIC

NIGHT LIFE

LATIN QUARTER

Flashy music and dance shows, vaudeville antics, famous stars, and beautiful women in various states of dress were what tourists expected of the New York nightclub scene and what Lou Walters' Latin Quarter delivered for over twenty-five years. Opening in 1942, this hot spot featured big names in show business over the years, such as Milton Berle, Sophie Tucker, Mae West, and Frank Sinatra. Lou Walters (father of Barbara Walters) was known for his ability to select showgirls who were to go on to further fame, such as Arlene Dahl, Irene Vernon, and Julie Wilson. It closed in 1969.

PICCADILLY CIRCUS BAR AT THE HOTEL PICCADILLY

The Piccadilly Circus Bar at the Hotel Piccadilly, "smartly located in the center of everything," was a modestly priced hotel bar near Times Square that featured a string ensemble during dinner and entertainment such as the Nevins Brothers and Arty Dunn in the 1940s, as advertised in this card. Frank J. Kennedy and his mixologists could conjure up all the popular cocktails of the day, such as New York City's very own concoctions the Bloody Mary and the Manhattan, starting at just thirty cents.

We're at the Sheraton Lounge! Where are You?

Hotel Sheraton
Lexington Ave. at 37th Street   New York City

HOTEL SHERATON GIRLS

The Hotel Sheraton, at Lexington Avenue and 37th Street, also had a lounge where guests and regulars could enjoy fine dining and drinking. The glamorous hostesses, known as Sheraton Girls, were an enticing part of the atmosphere and served "your favorite drink, mixed with a touch of genius . . . served with a touch of Venus."

HOTEL DIXIE PLANTATION BAR AND LOUNGE (TONY LANE AND THE AIRLANE TRIO)

TONY LANE AND THE AIRLANE TRIO
Appearing in the
HOTEL DIXIE PLANTATION BAR AND LOUNGE
No Cover - - No Minimum - - No Cabaret Tax

Advertising no cover or minimum, this Times Square hotel served hot hors d'oeuvres and "giant cocktails" in its Plantation Bar and Lounge in the 1950s. Entertainment included Hank Faller at the piano nightly with his original arrangements of the standards, and acts such as accordion-playing Tony Lane and the Airlane Trio, shown here.

COPACABANA

Plaza 8-0900

One of the longest-lasting nightclubs in the city, the Copacabana, at 10 East 60th Street, which opened in 1940, is probably the most famous, as well. June Allyson and Carroll Baker got their starts in this tropical oasis, and such greats as Frank Sinatra, Ella Fitzgerald, Nat King Cole, Jimmy Durante, and Joe E. Lewis performed there when they were in town. Another Copa favorite, "the Brazilian Bombshell," Carmen Miranda's colorful, fruity headpieces became the symbol for the nightclub. In 1960 Bobby Darin recorded "Darin at the Copa" there, but by that time the popularity of nightclubs was waning and this hot spot closed in the early 1970s.

STORK CLUB PRIVATE ROOM

The Stork Club, one of the most famous speakeasies-turned-legitimate at the end of Prohibition, was where the "in crowd" was seen. Newspaper columnist Walter Winchell frequented the club and was a good friend of owner Sherman Billingsley. Together they would sit in their booth near the bar, play cards, and determine which patrons should stay, where they should be seated, and who should be barred completely. As much as patrons wanted to get into the club, they were in good company if they were not let past the "golden rope": Humphrey Bogart and Jackie Gleason were two of the many not admitted to the club.

THIS IS JUST ONE OF THE NINE PRIVATE ROOMS AT THE STORK CLUB • CAPACITY 25 TO 500

THE FAMOUS HOLLYWOOD CABARET

Nils T. Granlund opened The Famous Hollywood Cabaret restaurant at Broadway and 48th Street around 1929. In the waning days of Prohibition, this nightclub offered a decent but inexpensive meal and entertained diners with nightly performances by glamorous starlets such as these. Granlund claimed his cabaret was the showplace of the World and was the originator of no cover charge.

THE ENSEMBLE OF "THE FAMOUS HOLLYWOOD CABARET" RESTAURANT, BROADWAY AT 48TH ST., NEW YORK CITY

HAWAIIAN ROOM, HOTEL LEXINGTON

The Hotel Lexington, at 48th Street, served Polynesian fare and had dancing and entertainment every night except Sunday in its Hawaiian Room. At this lavishly decorated club, authentic hula dancers from Hawaii were introduced in 1938, and entertainers such as Arthur Godfrey with his ukulele and Hilo Hattie with her rendition of "The Cockeyed Mayor of Kaunakakai" were featured. Other favorite acts included Andy Iona's Royal Hawaiians and Ray Kinney and the Aloha Maids, seen here. Though the hotel is still open, the Hawaiian Room is no longer in operation.

RAY KINNEY'S ORCHESTRA & ALOHA MAIDS · HAWAIIAN ROOM, HOTEL LEXINGTON, N.Y.C.

CLUB 18

With Heckler Jack's outlandish antics, every night at Jack White's Club 18 was raucous, hilarious, and unpredictable. The club was infamous for such pranks as dumping soup into women's laps and following men with a spotlight on their way to the lavatory. Sooner or later, all celebrities who passed through the doors were greeted with White's brash sense of humor, including the Chinese Ambassador who was invited as an honored guest and then was given a bag of dirty laundry.

"18" Club — JACK WHITE AND ALL THE GANG — 20 WEST 52ND ST. NEW YORK CITY

ROSELAND

Louis Brecker opened Roseland Ballroom for dancing and great music in the 1920s. His upscale "taxi dancers," called hostesses, worked the floor nightly, dancing with single men into the night for ten cents a whirl. Brecker insisted that the women be treated with respect and that customers were not allowed to engage the women after hours. The dress code was jackets and ties for men, which Brecker provided if necessary, and if any of the patrons got out of line, his "housemen" would escort them out of the ballroom. The original Roseland closed and was demolished in 1956; it reopened as the Roseland Dance City in 1957.

ROSELAND, "America's Foremost Ballroom"
Broadway at 51st Street, New York City

RESTAURANTS

PADDY'S CLAMHOUSE—215 W. 34TH ST

Paddy's Clamhouse, at 215 W. 34th Street, was the second restaurant of that name Joseph Patrick White opened in the city. White, who learned the restaurant trade at Delmonico's oyster bar, was famous for the world record he set in the early 1900s for opening clams— 100 of them in just three minutes, twenty seconds. Despite the no-frills, casual setting, patrons lined up on Sundays in the 1950s for his broiled lobster dinner that included an appetizer, French fries, green salad, dessert, and coffee or tea for just $2.55.

RUSSIAN BEAR

The first Russian restaurant to open in New York City was the Russian Bear, which began serving in 1908. Known for its authentic cuisine, decor reminiscent of the glory days of the empire, and its entertainment, this restaurant catered to an old-country clientele and was a popular spot for Russian émigrés and expatriates. Among the patrons was the famous revolutionary Leon Trotsky, who it is said dined there in 1917 during a brief stay in New York City before joining Lenin and the Bolshevik Revolution later that year.

PEOPLES OF RUSSIA

RUDI & MAXL'S BRAU-HAUS

Little Germany, the Yorkville neighborhood that centered around East 86th Street, was famous for its German and Hungarian restaurants, beer halls, and pastry shops and even featured a foreign-film theater specializing in German flicks. Always crowded, Rudi & Maxl's Brau-Haus had dancing and entertainment nightly and served such Bavarian favorites as kalbshaxen, pigs' knuckles, and sauerbraten. Of course, the beer flowed freely, too. The original Maxl's, just down the street at 243 East 68th Street, also featured singing waiters. During World War II, many of these establishments closed and the area's German flavor was lost.

FELTMAN'S FAMOUS RESTAURANT, CONEY ISLAND

For seventy-five years a trip out to Coney Island would not be complete without dining at Feltman's. Charles Feltman, who is reputed to have introduced the frankfurter to the U.S., opened this famous restaurant on Surf Avenue in 1871. As much an amusement park as a restaurant, it offered fresh seafood and, of course, hot dogs, at reasonable prices and had entertainment such as singers and dancers dressed in Bavarian garb and the Looff Carousel located in the beer garden. Despite this popularity, the restaurant declined along with the rest of Coney Island as an amusement destination during the depression and closed in 1946.

NINOS

Decorated in "hollyberry pink," a color introduced by Queen Elizabeth during a visit, and featuring Linzee Prescott's mural *Esprit Carnaval* (seen in this card), Nino's Ten East was known as one of the most expensive restaurants anywhere. Its exclusive Sports Afield Room seated only forty and offered the most exotic foods gathered from all around the world. Such rare delicacies as Moroccan octopus, Mexican armadillo, and Australian kangaroo were available with forty-eight hours notice. But there was a hefty price for this: a dinner for four could cost $100 per person and some entrees were as much as $55 in the 1950s.

REUBEN'S 6 E. 58TH STREET

German immigrant Arnold Reuben opened the first of his authentic delicatessens in New York City in 1908. By the time the third store at 6 East 58th Street opened in 1928, they were very popular with locals and tourists alike. Contrary to popular lore, the Reuben sandwich (corned beef on unseeded rye, with sauerkraut and Russian dressing) did not originate at Reuben's, though you certainly could have gotten one there until the last of the delis closed in 1966.

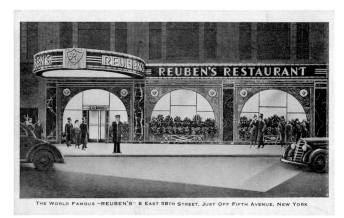

THE WORLD FAMOUS "REUBEN'S" 6 EAST 58TH STREET, JUST OFF FIFTH AVENUE, NEW YORK

WEISMANTEL'S SHOWBOAT

Offering fine dining, dancing, three "Broadway" revues nightly, and plenty of parking, Weismantel's Showboat in Cypress Hills, was a popular neighborhood place for dinner and catered functions such as weddings. While the restaurant did have the nautical presence of a ship, the artist of the Milwaukee company that produced this card took great liberties with the form of the building.

Weismantel's Showboat, 808-20 Jamaica Ave., Near Crescent St. (Telephone Applegate 7-9853) Cypress Hills, N. Y.

JACK DEMPSEY'S

Owned by the boxer after he retired from the ring, Jack Dempsey's Restaurant, at Broadway and 49th Street opposite Madison Square Garden, was a popular spot from its opening in 1935 until it closed in 1974. Most nights, Dempsey was at the restaurant greeting customers, posing for pictures, signing autographs, and telling stories about his famous bout with Willard, which was captured visually in the James Montogomery Flagg painting featured in the bar area. The artist of this postcard created a fantasy with it: the almost country-like setting, classy cars, and elegantly dressed people lend to the atmosphere but were from the artist's imagination.

"THE MEETING PLACE OF THE WORLD"

JACK DEMPSEY'S RESTAURANT, 50th St. at 8th Ave. Opp. Madison Square Garden, New York City

THEATRE

HIPPODROME—THE AEROPLANE BALLET IN "AMERICA"

Billed as the "Largest Company on the Largest Stage in the Largest Theatre in the World," the Hippodrome's production *America* ran for 360 performances in the years 1913—14. Historic events were the backdrop for this lavish spectacle, which opened with the landing of Columbus and covered the landscape of America at pivotal times, with such settings as a New England farm, the antebellum South, the Alamo, and the tenements and fashionable hotels of New York City. Other sketches were performed, such as the *Parasol Number* and the *Aeroplane Number,* depicted here.

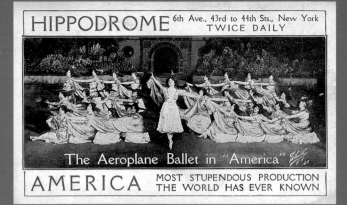

HIPPODROME 6th Ave., 43rd to 44th Sts., New York
TWICE DAILY

The Aeroplane Ballet in "America"

AMERICA — MOST STUPENDOUS PRODUCTION THE WORLD HAS EVER KNOWN

HIPPODROME

Occupying an entire block on 6th Avenue, with a seating capacity of 5,200, everything about the Hippodrome (opening in 1905) was on a grand scale. The stage was 200 feet wide and 100 feet deep (large enough for the jai-alai exhibition games played there), and it had a 60-foot apron that could be filled with water for aquatic productions. Behind the scenes, hydraulic machines raised and lowered the stage, and an indoor stable kept horses and elephants for the circus productions. The spectacles were so expensive to produce that the theater was not financially successful, however, and it closed in the late 1930s.

The Hippodrome, New York.

THE RIVOLI—BROADWAY AT 49TH ST.

Samuel L. "Roxy" Rothafel, the "genius of the movie palace," opened the Rivoli at Broadway and 49th Street on December 19, 1917, with the feature *A Modern Musketeer,* starring Douglas Fairbanks. The program Rothafel developed at the theater, featuring music, singing, a newsreel or short feature, and, finally, the movie, became a standard for movie theaters. The Rivoli survived into the 1980s but was not granted landmark status and was demolished in 1987.

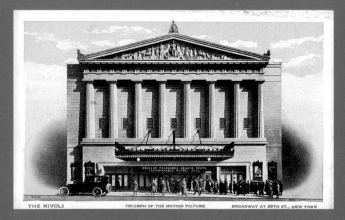

THE RIVOLI — TRIUMPH OF THE MOTION PICTURE — BROADWAY AT 49TH ST., NEW YORK

INTERIOR OF THE OLD METROPOLITAN OPERA HOUSE

In 1880, fed up with being shut out of the limited box seats of the old, aristocratic Academy of Music on Irving Place, such new millionaires as William H. Vanderbilt and Jay Gould fought back by founding the Metropolitan Opera House Company. The Metropolitan Opera House at Broadway and 39th Street opened its first season on October 2, 1883, with *Faust,* starring Italo Campanini. This space had very little backstage room for rehearsal and storage, and other locations were suggested over the years, including what became Rockefeller Center. Closing night was April 19, 1966, at this location. The next season, the opera reopened at Lincoln Center.

ROXY THEATER, 7TH AVE. AND 50TH ST.

When "Roxy" Rothafel opened the Roxy Theater in 1927, it was the largest theater of its kind in the world. With a price tag of $12 million and containing more than 6,000 seats, it was billed as a grand movie palace, but in typical Roxy style, elaborate live performances were also part of the show. The orchestra section seated 100 musicians, the ballet corps had up to 100 dancers, including the Gae Foster Roxyettes featured in this card. These high-stepping dancers were the forerunners of the Rockettes, who Roxy took with him when his contract with the theater expired and he moved his show to the Radio City Music Hall in 1932. The Roxy was razed in 1961.

SWEET BIRD OF YOUTH

This advertising card depicts a scene from the 1959 debut of Tennessee Williams' *Sweet Bird of Youth* to entice patrons to the performance. The back of it lists the prices for the show—as much as $6.90 for orchestra seats evenings and as little as $1.75 for the balcony for matinees—and also offers to mail the card if given to an usher. Starring Geraldine Page, Paul Newman, Sydney Blackmer, and Rip Torn, *Sweet Bird of Youth* opened in New York City at the Martin Beck Theatre on March 10, 1959.

PORGY & BESS

In the early 1900s, legitimate theaters in New York City used postcards like these to advertise their productions. This card for *Porgy and Bess* advises to "See it if you see nothing else," and suggests that the user of the card write a review of the production and mail it to a friend—a great way to promote the show. This revival of the 1935 opera by Du Bose Heyward and George Gershwin opened on January 22, 1942, at the Majestic Theatre and ran for eight months, setting a record for the longest-running revival on Broadway to that point.

George Gershwin and DuBose Heyward's "PORGY AND BESS" at the Majestic Theatre
"The town's bargain—with best seats at $2.75"—Walter Winchell

RADIO CITY MUSIC HALL

"Roxy" Rothafel continued with the live performance and movie format he made popular at his early venues when he came to Radio City Music Hall in 1932. Under this format, an afternoon or evening at the theater might include a stage show featuring the classically trained Corps de Ballet dancing to such works as *Rhapsody in Blue* and *Bolero,* the tap-inspired Rockettes, the Men's Glee Club, other variety acts, and a world premier of a motion picture. This format continued at Radio City until 1979.

GRAND FOYER

FAMOUS ROCKETTES

WORLD'S LARGEST THEATRE ORCHESTRA

GRAND LOUNGE

SECTION OF CORPS DE BALLET

New York City

Radio City Music Hall

K6739

SPORTS

SHEA STADIUM

Erected during the building boom of the 1964 New York World's Fair, Shea Stadium was constructed at a cost of $28.5 million, with motorized stands to allow it to be converted from a baseball diamond in the spring to a football gridiron in the fall. It was home to the New York Jets (1964–84) and the New York Giants (1973–75) until both football teams left New York City for Giants Stadium in East Rutherford, New Jersey.

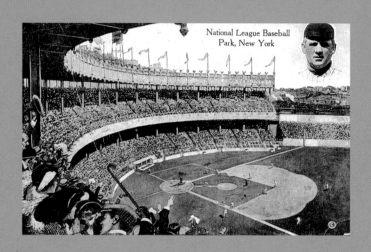

NATIONAL LEAGUE BASEBALL PARK

Known as the Polo Grounds—named after the former New York Giants field at 110th Street and 5th Avenue, where polo used to be played—the National League Baseball Park was home to the team from the time it was constructed in 1911 until 1957 when they moved to San Francisco. The Yankees played there as well from 1913 to 1922, and it was here that Babe Ruth hit his first professional home run and where such greats as Carl Hubbell, Mel Ott, and Willie Mays played. The face of John J. McGraw, manager of the Giants from 1902 to 1932, is visible on this card. After the Giants abandoned this field, the New York Mets played here from 1962 until 1963, when they moved to Shea, and the field was demolished a year later for the construction of apartment buildings.

EBBETS FIELD

The Brooklyn Dodgers won nine National League pennants at Ebbets Field during their tenure there (1913–57) but only one World Series (1955). On August 26, 1939, this park was the site of the first televised baseball game in history. It was also the site where, on April 15, 1947, Jackie Robinson, the first African-American baseball player in the major leagues, made his début as first baseman for the Dodgers. With all this history, indeed, it was a dark day in Brooklyn when Walter O'Malley moved "dem bums" to California in 1957. The field was demolished in 1960, and the famous scoreboard clock is now at McCormick Field in Asheville, North Carolina.

YANKEE STADIUM

Few structures in the city possess the rich history that Yankee Stadium does. Here, in the House the Ruth Built, heroes were made and records that are the hallmarks of baseball history were achieved and broken. Babe Ruth hit his sixtieth home run here, and Roger Maris broke his record decades later in the same park. Joltin' Joe DiMaggio began his fifty-six-game hitting streak here, and Mickey Mantle hit his 500th home run in 1967. It was also at Yankee Stadium that, in 1939, Lou Gehrig, "the Iron Horse," said good-bye to the game—in the same field where he began his infamous 2,130-consecutive-game streak in 1925. The park was renovated in the 1970s and continues to be the home of the World Champion Yankees.

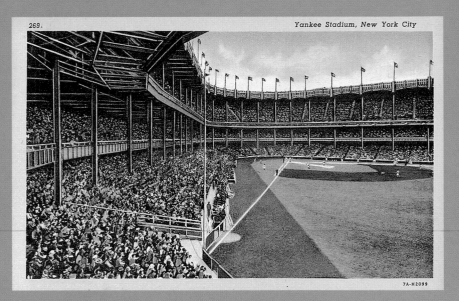

269.   Yankee Stadium, New York City

7A-H2099

MADISON SQUARE GARDEN, NEW YORK CITY

MADISON SQUARE GARDEN

This Madison Square Garden at 8th Avenue and 49th Street opened in 1925 and was the third "Garden" to use the name. It was built by Tex Rickard, a sports promoter, who brought boxing to the old Madison Square Garden and made it flourish at this new location. Though it was successful for decades, the facility went into decline and closed in 1966 at this location. In 1968 it reopened at its current location atop Pennsylvania Station.

71

MADISON SQUARE GARDEN
(WITH SPORTING EVENTS)

While the first two Madison Square Gardens were more about theater and other types of events, the third Garden was all about sports. The sporting events popularized at the Garden were boxing with such greats as Jack Dempsey, hockey with the Rangers, professional basketball with the Knicks, and college basketball, but it also catered to a broader audience by hosting such productions as ice shows, the circus, rodeos, and annual horse and bike events.

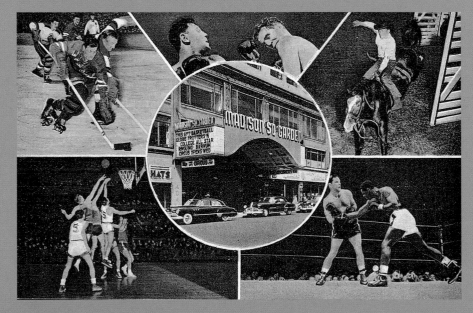

ICELAND SKATING RINK
(Adj. Madison Sq. Garden)
8TH. AVE. & 50TH. ST., N.Y.C.

ICELAND SKATING RINK

Catering to the crowds drawn by the newly opened Madison Square Garden at 8th Avenue and 49th Street, the Iceland Skating Rink was one of the most elegant and popular ice rinks to open in the 1920s. Skaters could whirl around the rink to a live orchestra, dine in the facility's restaurant, attend ice shows, take lessons from instructors, and even rent lockers and skates.

RECREATION PIER

The first recreation pier on the East River opened in 1897 at the foot of East 3rd Street, and as its popularity grew, five more followed along the this river and the Hudson. In the days when there were few designated parks to escape to, these piers were built as a place for urban inhabitants to get away from the often overcrowded, unpleasant conditions of the city and have a clean, safe place to enjoy a little fresh air. They were a most popular play area for children during the day, and at night, adults enjoyed quiet walks along the piers.

Recreation Pier, New York.

Designed for the Pleasure of Skating

Queens and **Horace Harding Boulevards**

One block from 8th Avenue Subway [Woodhaven Bl'vd Sta.]

QUEENS ROLLER RINK

Located on Queens and Horace Harding Boulevards in Elmherst, the Queens Roller Rink was one of the largest skating rinks in New York in the 1950s. This advertising card was good for a free admission for a couple (lady and gentleman) for an evening of skating and enticed patrons with a description of its "complete sound proof construction—affording every possible advantage of the full tonal benefits from the Hammond Organ and Novacord."

TODT HILL

Called "Iron Hill" by the Dutch, Todt Hill, at 410 feet above sea level, is the highest point of land on the Atlantic seaboard south of Maine. One of the persistent stories for this unusual name is that it is a variation of "Toad Hill." In the eighteenth century, so the story goes, a young woman, wishing to spurn the advances of a suitor, surreptitiously slipped toads into the pocket of his coat. For some time after, his friends chided him about the incident, and the hill where the young woman lived became known as "Toad Hill." The golf course pic-

TODT HILL, STATEN ISLAND, N. Y. "HIGHEST POINT ON COAST FROM MAINE TO FLORIDA"   3

tured here eventually became part of "the Greenbelt," a group of six parks in Staten Island.

SIGHTSEEING

The "Islander" - One of the Sightseeing Yachts in the Circle Line Fleet

THE ISLANDER—
ONE OF THE SIGHTSEEING YACHTS
IN THE CIRCLE LINE FLEET

Founded in 1945, the Circle Line originally circled Manhattan Island clockwise but switched to counterclockwise later on. Early converted yachts in the Circle Line fleet, like the one in this postcard, had names such as the *Traveler, Visitor, Islander* and *Tourist* and were replaced by LCIs originally used during World War II for transporting troops to enemy-held positions along foreign shorelines.

WILSON LINE—"MODERN EXCURSION VESSEL"

Not just for out-of-town tourists, excursion vessels offered a means for locals to travel to cities and recreational sites in the vicinity and up the Hudson River. These day liners, such as the Wilson Line ship depicted here, were popular until 1989 with church groups heading out for picnics both on the boat itself and destinations along the river as far as Albany. This card is an invitation to join St. Luke's Episcopal Church aboard the *State of Pennsylvania* for a trip to Bear Mountain on August 23, 1952. This ship offered such amenities as the ability to accommodate over 3,000 people, a large ballroom for dancing, a cocktail bar, and refreshments.

MODERN NEW YORK EXCURSION VESSEL

8B-H391

8942. "SEEING NEW YORK."

"SEEING NEW YORK"—STARTS FROM FLATIRON BLDG.

In the nineteenth century, as the city grew, so did tourism. By the turn of the last century, tour companies such as the Royal Blue Line, with its fleet of nine electric busses like the one depicted here, offered tours of Manhattan and Brooklyn as one way of "Seeing New York." Companies such as the Gray Line and Apple Tours have continued this means of touring the city.

NEW YORK SKYLINE AS SEEN FROM FERRY BOAT

The Staten Island Ferry, plying the waters between Manhattan and Staten Island, has long been considered the best way to see the sights of the harbor and with its low price, " the best deal in town." Until 1974 the ride cost pedestrians five cents, and the fares increased to fifty cents in 1989. On July 4, 1997, Mayor Rudolph Giuliani abolished the fee. A generous gesture, to be sure, but hardly the bargain it was at five cents.

182:—NEW YORK SKYLINE AS SEEN FROM A FERRYBOAT.

44250

MUSEUMS

MUSEUM OF MODERN ART, E. 53RD STREET, NEW YORK CITY

44   14838

MUSEUM OF MODERN ART

In 1929, Lillie P. Bliss, Abby Aldrich Rockefeller and Mary Quinn Sullivan founded the Museum of Modern Art to encourage and promote the schools of modern art developing abroad. The museum's 1939 modern glass-and-steel building stands in contrast to the thirty-foot Alaskan totem pole. Made of red cedar and carved with the faces of a raven, a killer whale, a fish, a sea lion, and a shark, it was erected in conjunction with an exhibition of Native American art in 1940.

MUSEUM OF NON-OBJECTIVE PAINTING

Founded by Solomon R. Guggenheim, the Museum of Non-Objective Painting opened at 24 East 54th Street in 1937 and featured works by Wassily Kandinsky and Paul Klee, among others. As the collection grew, Guggenheim determined that his museum should be in the most prominent place in town, Fifth Avenue. He commissioned Frank Lloyd Wright to design the building in 1943 and it was completed in 1959. Oddly, this is the only building in New York City by the famed architect.

MUSEUM OF NON-OBJECTIVE PAINTING — 24 EAST 54TH STREET, NEW YORK CITY
SOLOMON R. GUGGENHEIM FOUNDATION

METROPOLITAN MUSEUM OF ART

The Metropolitan Museum of Art was founded in 1870 by leading New York citizens wishing to have a museum in the city that which rivaled those grand museums in Europe. The first building, which opened in 1880, was created by Central Park designer Calvert Vaux and architect Jacob Wrey Mould. The blocks at the tops of the four Corinthian columns that form the main entrance of the later Fifth Avenue facade visible in this card, were to bear carved figures reflecting the four great periods of art—Egyptian, Greek, Renaissance and Modern—but this was never completed.

Metropolitan Museum of Art, New York

HAYDEN PLANETARIUM

At the time it was built in 1935, the Hayden Planetarium was a state-of-the-art facility. Its Zeiss projector, designed specifically for the building, showed the movement of 9,000 stars from both hemispheres and the rising and setting of the sun and moon. *The Star of Christmas* show featured a view of the stars over Bethlehem on the night Jesus was born and was a popular attraction during the holiday season. Deemed out-of-date, and despite its designation as a landmark, the structure was demolished in the late 1990s to build the current Rose Center for Earth and Space.

77

155:—THE HAYDEN PLANETARIUM, NEW YORK CITY.

SKYSCRAPERS

The term skyscraper was used in the eighteenth century to refer to the tallest mast on a ship, but as the buildings of Manhattan grew towards the sky, it came to be applied to them. Two nineteenth-century innovations made them possible. Inventor Elisha G. Otis demonstrated his steam-powered passenger elevator at New York's Crystal Palace in 1852, and this technology enabled both construction workers and inhabitants of these increasingly tall structures to easily travel from floor to floor. The second innovation, steel-cage frame construction, enabled buildings to be built with an internal steel structure for support. Prior to this, the outside walls of the buildings supported it, so they had to be very thick at the bottom to sustain the upper floors, limiting the height of the structure. The first building in New York to employ steel structure, the World Tower Building (1889), was built by Bradford Gilbert Lee, who placed his office on the top floor to prove a building constructed in this manner was safe. This building, at 50 Broadway, was demolished just fourteen years later to make way for an even taller structure.

BROOKLYN BRIDGE AND WOOLWORTH BUILDING, NEW YORK CITY.

TRINITY CHURCH

Though not a skyscraper in the strict sense, the 281-foot steeple of Trinity Church, the third church to be built on the spot, was designed by Richard Upjohn in 1846 and reigned as the tallest structure in Manhattan until construction of the Brooklyn Bridge towers began in the 1870s. The churchyard is the final resting place for many famous people, including Alexander Hamilton, who died of wounds received in his infamous duel with Aaron Burr, Captain James "don't give up ship" Lawrence, and steamboat inventor Robert Fulton, who is entombed in the Livingston vault.

BROOKLYN BRIDGE

At 276 feet above and 78 feet below the high-water mark, the Manhattan Tower of the Brooklyn Bridge became the tallest structure in New York when it was completed in 1876. The opening of the bridge on May 24, 1883, was met with great fanfare. Six days after this, the bridge was the scene of a tragic event. According to accounts, a panicked mob of pedestrians on the bridge who believed it was collapsing after they heard a woman's scream stampeded, trampling twelve people to death and injuring more than thirty. A year later, P. T. Barnum declared it was safe after parading twenty-one pachyderms across it.

Trinity Church and Skyscrapers at Night, New York.

19623

WORLD TOWER BUILDING. NEW YORK CITY.

WORLD BUILDING

At 309 feet high, the gold-domed World Building, also known as the Pulitzer Building, was the tallest in the world when it was completed in 1890. Designed by George B. Post, this building was built for Joseph B. Pulitzer, publisher of the *Evening World*. After his death in 1911 the newspaper declined but remained in publication until 1931 when it merged into the *Telegram*. The building remained an office building and a fixture on Park Row until it was demolished in the 1960s.

PARK ROW BUILDING

When the Park Row Building, at 390 feet, was completed in 1899, it surpassed the World Building as the tallest in New York. It wasn't, however, the tallest structure in the world: both the Eiffel Tower and the Cologne Cathedral were higher. The builder of this twin-turreted tower was August Belmont, a wealthy banker who was also instrumental in the construction of the subway system shortly after. The building received landmark status in 1999, and there are currently plans to convert the top floors to apartments while keeping the bottom floors commercial (center card right).

SINGER BUILDING

Ernest T. Flagg's Singer Tower became the world's tallest building for one year when it was completed in 1908. At 612 feet, this building had sixteen elevators that took visitors up to the forty-second-floor observation area in a minute for just fifty cents. Several suicides from this high vantage point led to the closure of this tourist attraction. This building, with a foundation consisting of thirty-six caissons sunk ninety-two feet below the surface into bedrock, was the tallest building and one of the most difficult ever to be demolished (in 1967).

METROPOLITAN LIFE BUILDING

Built in 1909, the Metropolitan Life Insurance Company Building, at 657 feet, was the tallest building in the world for four years. The four-faced clock on the tower is 26-$\frac{1}{2}$ feet in diameter and the dials are two stories high. Before the tower's completion, during the 1908 presidential election, a large searchlight was placed on top of it that told the election results for miles around.

WOOLWORTH BUILDING

As Singer found when he built his tower in 1908, the "tallest building" race was important as an advertisement for the strength of a company. When Woolworth attempted to borrow money from the

PARK ROW, NEW YORK. *Morris Campbell*

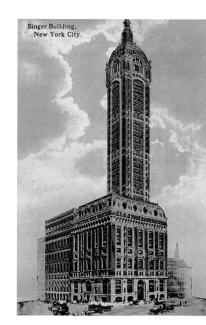

Singer Building, New York City.

Looking up Park

Metropolitan Life Insurance Company to build his corporate headquarters, they would not lend it to him, and so, in revenge, he was determined to have his building grow taller than Met Life's. Cass Gilbert's Gothic structure, complete with turrets and gargoyles, did just that in 1913, topping out at 792 ½ feet (center card left).

BANK OF MANHATTAN BUILDING

William H. Reynolds, the real estate developer responsible for the fanciful Dream Land Park at Coney Island, was the creator of the Chrysler Building completed in 1930. Its architect, William Van Allen, was caught up in a competition with his ex-partner, H. Craig Severance, who was building the Bank of Manhattan Company's building at 40 Wall Street at the same time. The plans for the Chrysler Building called for it to be 925 feet high, so Severance decided to add a flagpole on top of his building to make it two feet taller. Little did he know that Van Allen was secretly building "the vertex"—the top spire, which he had assembled inside the building. When this was attached to the top, it put his building's height at 1,038 feet.

CHRYSLER BUILDING

Famous for the Cloud Club (closed in 1979), which boasted an exclusive dining room, overnight accommodations for special guests, and a men's room with the best view in town, the distinctive art deco dome of the Chrysler Building was also where, in 1940, the transmission of the first color-television broadcast occurred.

EMPIRE STATE BUILDING

Toppling the Chrysler Building's reign as tallest building in the world after just eleven months, the Empire State Building (1,472 feet), with a daily construction force of over 2,500 men, took only thirteen months to complete and is still regarded as the fastest-rising skyscraper in the world. It opened May 1, 1931, and for numerous years during the depression it was known as "the Empty State Building" because much of it remained unoccupied. The spire at the top was originally intended to be a dirigible mooring mast but dangerous updrafts and high winds made this unfeasible. The Empire State Building remained the tallest building in the world until the completion of the twin towers of the World Trade Center (1,250 feet) in the 1970s.

ON THE GO

Underground R. R. and Brooklyn Bridge Terminal, New York.

CITY HALL STATION

The same architects who designed the Cathedral of St. John the Divine were responsible for the City Hall Station, and with its skylights, chandeliers, and intricate tile work it is still considered the most elegant subway station in the city. The first subway ride occurred here on October 24, 1904, when Mayor McClellan and other city officials traveled to 42nd Street and Lexington Avenue and then across to Times Square and up Broadway to 143rd Street. The station was closed in 1945 because it was considered too small to accommodate the large number of passengers using the subway by that time.

UNDERGROUND RR AND BROOKLYN BRIDGE TERMINAL

The large train sheds visible in this card were used for the elevated trains that ran over the bridge between Brooklyn and Manhattan. The elevated tracks were on either side of the pedestrian walkway, and service began for these in 1883 and ended in 1944. Also visible in this card is the domed World, or "Pulitzer," Building. This twenty-six-story structure, built in 1890 and once the tallest building in the world, was demolished in the early 1950s to increase vehicular access to the bridge.

ELEVATED CURVE AT 110TH STREET

Standing at one hundred feet high, the 110th Street curve, dismantled in 1940, was the highest point along the elevated line. Averaging about thirty feet high, the elevated was a boon to commuters because it allowed them to move swiftly over the congested city streets and contributed to the populating of northern Manhattan and beyond. But it was also very dangerous. In the early days before the trains were electric, the smoke as well as falling embers and dripping oil were hazardous to those in the vicinity of the tracks.

Elevated R. R. Curve at 110th Street, New York.

INTERIOR OF ELEVATED CAR

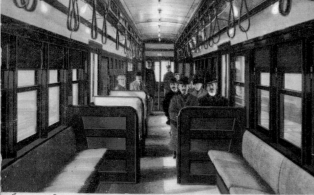

Interior of Elevated Car.

The elegantly appointed Pullman cars used on the elevated tracks in the early days of mass transportation featured cane seating, oak paneling, and mahogany molding. In the nineteenth century a varied price system was in place for the elevated. Fares were as low as five cents during rush hour and up to twenty cents for a ride in one of the 3rd Avenue line's "drawing room cars" that ran along the Upper East Side. For ten cents you were legally entitled to a seat, and if there was not one available, it was your right to travel for free.

HUDSON TUNNELS,
Entrance from Lackawanna Station, Hoboken Terminal

HUDSON TUNNELS — 14TH ST. & 6TH AVE.

Prior to the Hudson Tunnels, the only way to get to Manhattan from New Jersey was to take one of the numerous ferries that clogged the busy seaport area. In 1908, commuters to the city hailed the completion of this project, and within twenty-four hours of the commencement of regular train service, fifty thousand riders had abandoned the slow ferry service for the eight-minute train trip to Lower Manhattan. When the Port of New York Authority took over the tunnels in 1962, this commuter system became the Port Authority Trans-Hudson Corporation (PATH).

Holland Vehicular Tunnel, New York City.

HOLLAND VEHICULAR TUNNEL

The first underwater vehicular tunnel and the longest tunnel in the world when it opened in 1927, the Holland Tunnel was the initial major project for the newly formed Port of New York Authority. The largest problem facing engineers was how to get the toxic automobile exhaust out of the tunnels. Chief engineer Clifford M. Holland is credited as having solved this by engineering an innovative air exchange system whereby fresh air is blown into the space underneath the roadway and vented through slits in the curb, and the exhaust from the cars is drawn out of the tunnel through the four ventilation towers. So innovative was Holland's creation, it became a model for vehicular tunnels worldwide.

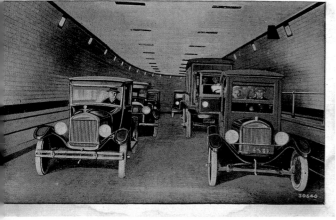

PORT AUTHORITY BUS TERMINAL
Eighth Avenue at Forty-first Street, New York City

One block from Times Square

PORT AUTHORITY BUS TERMINAL

Spanning two blocks on 8th Avenue between 40th and 42nd Streets, the Port Authority Bus Terminal, depicted here before subsequent renovations, was the largest mass-transit center of its kind in the world when it opened in December 1950. It offered such amenities as heated on- and off-ramps to melt snow, air-conditioned telephone booths, redcap service, and telephones on walls near terminal entrances, which allowed customers immediate access to "information girls" who could give departure, fare, tax, and routing schedules almost instantaneously.

160   Lincoln Tunnel between Weehawken, N. J. and New York City

LINCOLN TUNNEL

The Port Authority Bus Terminal uses the Port Authority-owned Lincoln Tunnel as its main artery into and out of Manhattan and is located close enough to Times Square and Penn Station and subways for commuters to easily access all areas in the city. And for people using buses to travel to points outside of the city, this facility offers a central location for their departure. For many years, the tunnel employed traffic guards who could be seen in their kiosks and patrolling along the catwalks on either side of the traffic.

LaGuardia Airport

Built in 1937, in a joint venture between the city and the WPA, LaGuardia Airport was constructed to facilitate the pending 1939 New York World's Fair in Flushing, Queens. In an effort to make it more financially successful, the airport encouraged New Yorkers to come to the field for inexpensive entertainment. A modest fee was charged to enter the Aviation Terrace, where one could have a Planter's Punch and watch the "great sky-birds" carrying celebrities arrive and depart. In addition, other concessions such as elegant restaurants, hair salons, and boutiques opened up to accommodate travelers.

Newark Airport

Newark Airport played a significant role in the early days of aviation history. Opening in 1928 on sixty-eight acres of marshland, it was the busiest airport in the world until LaGuardia opened ten years later. Every weekend the airport sponsored air shows, and it was here that many of the first demonstrations of new airplanes and the early flight record attempts, such as those of Charles Lindbergh, Howard Hughes, and Amelia Earhart, took place. Newark also served as the easternmost terminus for transcontinental airmail and the hub of other international cargo shipments.

Floyd Bennett Field

Floyd Bennett Field on Jamaica Bay, created in 1931, was the first municipal airport in New York City. Named after the pilot who flew Admiral Richard E. Byrd over the North Pole in 1926, it was popular with famous aviators such as Laura Ingalls, Douglas "Wrongway" Corrigan, and John Glenn, and was host to such air races as the Bendix Trophy Race. But due to its failure to attract the U.S. Postal Service business away from Newark, it did not become a viable commercial venture. The airport, with its seaplane base, was eventually leased to the Coast Guard in 1936 and later the U.S. Navy. By 1941, all commercial use of the airport was discontinued.

Hotel New Yorker Aviation Terrace   LaGuardia Field

Newark Airport, Newark, N. J.

FLOYD BENNETT FIELD, BROOKLYN, N. Y.

PHOTO BY RUDY ARNOLD

THE NINETEEN THIRTY-NINE NEW YORK WORLD'S FAIR

TRYLON AND PERISPHERE

Built on an ash dump in Flushing, Queens, the New York World's Fair of 1939 was a symbol of optimism for the future. This vision of the World of Tomorrow opened in April 1939, and by the time it closed in October 1940, close to forty-five million people had visited it. Pavilions sponsored by foreign nations and companies were set up to expose visitors to the broader world and emerging future technologies that were to shape every facet of their lives. On display were such advances as FM radio, robotics, television, and even a fax machine. The most popular exhibit was General Motors' Futurama, which featured a eerily prophetic vision of the future America in 1960, focusing on the exodus of city dwellers to the suburbs, and the advent of miles of highway and cars required to make this possible. Visible in this postcard is the symbol for the fair, the Theme Center, which consisted of the 700-foot-tall Trylon (the Pointer to Infinity), and the 200-foot-diameter Perisphere (the World of Tomorrow), which was encircled by the Helicline, a 950-foot walkway.

Dear:
We just saw these little Sunshine Bakers at the Loose Wiles Biscuit Co.
Exhibit at the New York World's Fair! They're the cutest little midgets you
ever saw and they put on a grand show!
Sincerely,

SUNSHINE BISCUITS

The Food Zone, where the Sunshine Bakers performed, was one of the seven zones at the fair that also included Government, Transportation, Communications, Community Interests, Production and Distribution, and the Amusement Zone. Other interesting exhibits in the Food Zone included the Borden display, where 150 cows were mechanically milked, and the Wonder Bakery described below. The front of this card reads: "Dear   , We just saw these little Sunshine Bakers at the Loose Wiles Biscuit Co. Exhibit at the New York World's Fair! They're the cutest little midgets you ever saw and they put on a grand show!"

SSW   Trylon and Perisphere, New York World's Fair

© N. Y. W. F.

Greetings from New York World's Fair

ENTRANCE TO THE BRITISH PAVILION.

ENTRANCE TO THE BRITISH PAVILION

In the Government Zone, where a visitor could "circle the globe in a single afternoon," close to sixty countries had pavilions displaying the distinct attributes of their cultures, including museum works and foods. Located on Presidential Row South, the British Pavilion exhibited a replica of the crown jewels, ceremonial plates, coins, parliamentary documents, and other antiques.

THE WONDER BAKERY, NEW YORK WORLD'S FAIR 1939

P. J. 2437

THE WONDER BAKERY

This modern bakery displayed the newest in technologies in baking and, through the Alice in Wonderland–themed pavilion, visitors could follow every step of the mechanized bread-making process from the sifting of flour, to the mixing of ingredients, to the rising process, to the baking, the slicing, and the packaging of the final product. The exhibit included a wheat field, the first one planted in New York City in nearly seventy years, and the Wonder Sandwich Bar, where visitors could sample the results of this process.

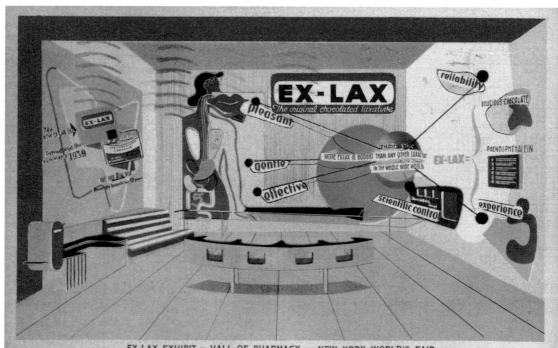

EX-LAX EXHIBIT — HALL OF PHARMACY — NEW YORK WORLD'S FAIR

Ex-Lax Exhibit — Hall of Pharmacy

The Hall of Pharmacy, in the Production and Distribution Zone, was divided into three parts: pharmaceutical chemistry, the medicine cabinet, and the drugstore of tomorrow, complete with a soda fountain of the future. Other exhibits in the zone included the General Electric exhibit, which featured a generator capable of artificially producing lightning and thunder.

Smoke Havana Cigars

The Cuban exhibit at the fair focused on the vast agricultural wealth of the country. Products such as sugar cane, tropical fruits, vegetables, and, of course, "the world's finest tobacco," were featured. The back of this card advises the prospective connoisseur of fine cigars to "look for the green Warranty Stamp of the Cuban Government" when selecting tobacco products and reminds the consumer that, in those pre-Castro days, "Seventy-five percent of its imports are from the United States."

14-ton Giant Underwood Master

The Giant Underwood Master typewriter, at 1,728 times larger than a normal-sized Underwood, typed out letters on 9 x 12 foot stationery with a ribbon 100 feet long and 5 inches wide and a carriage weighing close to two tons. During the fair, George L. Hossfield and Grace Phelan, professional and amateur championship typists, respectively, gave demonstrations on regular-sized Underwoods.

THE 14-TON GIANT UNDERWOOD MASTER
OPERATING DAILY
AT THE NEW YORK WORLD'S FAIR 1939

ADVERTISING CARDS

Since their inception, color-illustrated postcards have been a popular and successful form of advertising for both large companies and individual establishments. Many of these clever and creative cards were produced in short runs, making them rare and valuable collector cards. Advertising cards can be found throughout this book, but featured in this chapter are some other wonderful and distinctive examples of this medium.

SOFIA—WORLD'S TALLEST STORAGE WAREHOUSE

Originally built as an elevatored garage, the Sofia Brothers Warehouse, "Tops in Storage," at 45 Columbus Avenue, was completed in 1930. This fabulously ornamental art deco warehouse is still standing but was converted into apartments in 1985.

World's Tallest Storage Warehouse
Main Office: 45 Columbus Avenue, New York City

WHEN IN NEW YORK VISIT FANNY FARMER

Once landmarks like the more famous ones featured on this postcard, the Fanny Farmer candy shops were a ubiquitous city institution. Fanny Farmer Candies, established in 1919, was named for Fanny Merrit Farmer, author of *The Fanny Farmer Cookbook* (1896). Before refrigeration became available in the late 1930s, the shops needed to be within 200 miles of their "studio," or manufacturing center, so that the highest-quality candy could be distributed. One of these studios was in New York City. The latticework visible on the building on this card was part of their signature look.

MOLNAR BEAUTY SPECIALISTS

This card, postmarked 1950, was created to appeal specifically to women and depicts a modern, elegant salon where a person of leisure might go to be pampered. Its message reads, "You and your friends are cordially invited to attend the 44th Anniversary celebration of our beauty salon where expert operators will serve you beauty at its very best. The latest in hair styling, shaping, permanent waving, and hair tinting can be yours. May we be *permanently* yours, Molnar Beauty Specialists."

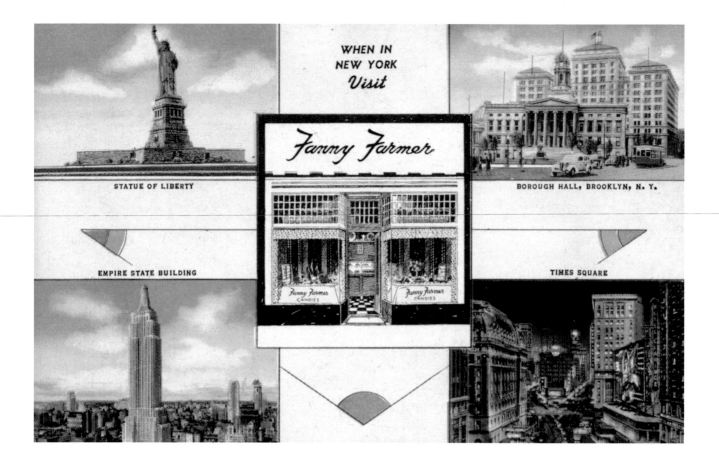

STATUE OF LIBERTY

WHEN IN
NEW YORK
Visit

Fanny Farmer

BOROUGH HALL, BROOKLYN, N. Y.

EMPIRE STATE BUILDING

TIMES SQUARE

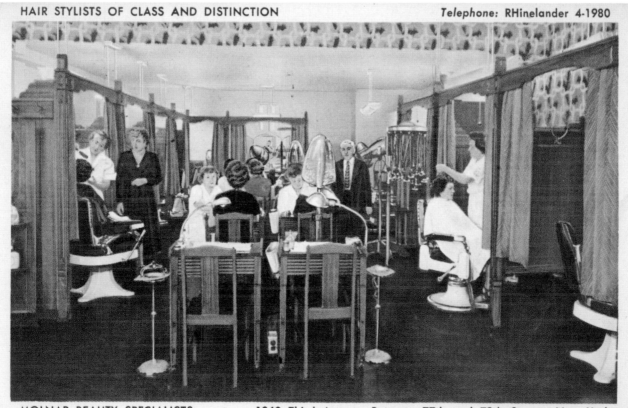

HAIR STYLISTS OF CLASS AND DISTINCTION   Telephone: RHinelander 4-1980

MOLNAR BEAUTY SPECIALISTS   •   1360 Third Avenue, Between 77th and 78th Streets, New York

QUIZ KIDS

Produced in the NBC Studios from 1949 to 1956, this popular game show consisted of a panel of five children who answered questions proposed by the viewing audience. The children could be as young as six and were allowed to remain on the show, earning a $100 savings bond each week, for as long as their answer rank remained high, or until they reached the age of sixteen. If a viewer's question stumped the panel, the viewer won a prize. This post-card is a notice of rejection for Mrs. Arthur Russell, on Staten Island, who submitted a question that was not chosen for the show.

HOTEL VICTORIA

As the newly constructed Rockefeller Center embodied many of the themes of the 1939 New York World's Fair, it was highly advertised as a destination for those in town for the fair. The Hotel Victoria, adjacent to the center, offered such modern amenities as a radio, a shower, and circulating ice water, as advertised in this card, as well as a free library and a rooftop golf course.

RK — SUNDAY AFTERNOONS — 4 o'clock E.S.T. —
— 2 o'clock Mountain — 1 o'clock Pacific Coast

ALKA-SELTZER AND ONE-A-DAY (Brand) VITAMINS

HOTEL BRISTOL

Typical of hotel postcards, this one advertising the Hotel Bristol gives a highly stylized view of the city. With the hotel as its focal point and the major landmarks that might appeal to visitors arranged around it, this card creates the illusion that the hotel was at the center of everything.

AUTOMAT

The Philadelphia-based company Horn & Hardart introduced New Yorkers to the automat in 1912. The clinking sound of nickels hitting the slots of the coffee machine, along with the immediacy of buns, sandwiches, casseroles, and slices of pie awaiting the diner through the characteristic glass doors appealed greatly to city dwellers constantly on the go. The automats were at their peak of popularity from the 1930s through 1950s; but as fast-food restaurants increased in the 1970s, the popularity of automats declined until 1991 when the last one closed.

VANDERBILT HOTEL'S MOTHER GOOSE PLAYROOM

The elegant and ornate Vanderbilt Hotel on Park Avenue and 34th Street, completed in 1912, was converted to office and apartment space in the 1960s. This card was produced not as an advertisement for the hotel itself, but rather for the Helen Speer Company, the designer and decorator of the Mother Goose Playroom. The solicitation on the back reads, "Please send me a set of your color plates illustrating your individual treatments of Children's Play Rooms."

GRAND CENTRAL THEATRE

Opening in 1937, the 242-seat Grand Central Theatre, at the eastern end of the Main Concourse, entertained those waiting for trains with cartoons, shorts, and current newsreels, a forerunner of CNN or Bloomberg News today. A clock was visible next to the screen so patrons could avoid missing their trains. This space, which had been obscured by a retail store, was uncovered during the recent renovations to the terminal and now contains a wine shop.

SPECIAL EFFECTS

ADD-ONS

Before natural color printing was prevalent in the publishing industry, the process by which postcards such as the white-bordered ones in this section were made was a lengthy one. The publishing firm would most often present the client with an actual photograph of the subject, possibly touched up to remove unsightly elements like telephone wires or signs. Using a color chart, the client would pick the colors appropriate for the card. An artist at the publishing company would then create a hand-drawn color sketch based on the photograph, adding embellishments as desired or requested, and this would be presented again to the client. Upon approval, press proofs would be created, and upon approval of these, the final printing would begin. Cards were often printed by the gang-run method, where numerous cards from various clients were printed together on the same sheet. Running the presses was expensive and this method allowed for multiple clients to contribute to the run, thereby reducing the cost.

95

HOLLAND TUNNEL AND SKY LINE
In an effort to keep motorists abiding by the thirty-mile-an-hour speed limit in the Holland Tunnel, as well as to report accidents and other trouble in the tunnel, catwalks along either side of the roadway were patrolled by guards, as reflected in this card. By the 1970s, an electronic sensing system that could monitor the traffic flow was added, and the guards were no longer needed. This card, with its fictitious skyline and other added elements, is most likely completely the work of the artist's imagination.

Zeppelin Flying Over City Hall Park, New York.

ZEPPELIN FLYING OVER CITY HALL PARK

City Hall Park was once one of the city's most important civic gathering places and was the site of the first public reading in New York City of the Declaration of Independence, which was witnessed by George Washington, among others. The unusual low building at the left is not an add-on, as are the dirigible and the plane, but rather the General Post Office, which sat at the south end of the park from 1878 until it was demolished in the late 1930s.

RITZ TOWER BUILDING

RITZ TOWER BUILDING, PARK AVE. & 57TH ST., NEW YORK

The Ritz Tower Building, at 540 feet, was the tallest residential building in the world when it was completed in 1925. It was leased by the Ritz-Carlton Hotel group and, like their hotels in London, Paris, and on Madison Avenue, it embodied the characteristics of wealth, luxury, and elegance that defined the phrase "puttin' on the Ritz." As indicated in the lower left corner, the original photograph on which this card is based was taken by the well-known New York photographer Irving Underhill. The biplane added on to this card gives the illusion of height to the forty-two-story tower.

GRANT'S TOMB

This 150-foot monument, a popular tourist destination even before Groucho Marx asked the question "Who's buried in Grant's Tomb?" was completed in 1897, twelve years after the general died. Contained in its two marble sarcophagi are the remains of Grant and his wife, Julia, who died in 1902. Day and night cards like these allowed postcard companies to reuse views and present them as new. Often doing no more than coloring the background to make a night view, this card is much more elaborate with the addition of the moon, spotlights shinning from the boats on the river, and elaborate lighting effects illuminating the automobiles and the tomb itself.

GRANT'S TOMB AND HUDSON RIVER BY MOONLIGHT, NEW YORK.

Grant's Tomb, New York.

ARCHITECTURAL ANOMALIES

In a hurry to get postcards in the consumers' hands while topics were hot and before the other publishers got to them first, postcard companies created cards based on plans and models of buildings that were not yet completed. Sometimes the structures were not built as originally designed and the results of this haste make fascinating historical documents, some of which appear in this section.

INTERSTATE HUDSON RIVER BRIDGE, (WEST APPROACH) CONNECTING N. Y. CITY AND NEW JERSEY STATE 2

4437-29

INTERSTATE HUDSON RIVER BRIDGE, WEST APPROACH

In the original plans for the George Washington Bridge, engineer Othmar H. Ammann and designer Cass Gilbert had intended that the steel structures of the two towers be covered with granite, in homage to the rocky cliffs of the adjacent Palisades, as reflected in this card. But due to financial difficulties of the depression, this was not completed when the first level opened in October 1931.

YANKEE STADIUM

The first site suggested for Yankee Stadium when the team decided to move from the Polo Grounds was 8th Avenue and 33rd Street, atop the Pennsylvania Railroad tracks, but this being nixed by the War Department, land was purchased just across the river from the old stadium in the Bronx. In its original plans for the first three-tier stadium built in America, the Osborn Engineering Company called for the top deck of Yankee Stadium to be covered completely, as reflected in this card, but this never got off the drawing board. This stadium, with a seating capacity of 75,000, was completed after 284 days of construction in 1922 at a cost of almost $3 million. It was renovated in the 1970s.

NEW COURT HOUSE

Depicted in this card is the proposed plan for the circular New York County Court House, now the New York State Supreme Court, designed by Guy Lowell in 1912. Due to financial constraints, a smaller, hexagonal structure was ultimately placed on Foley Square in 1927. The courthouse rotunda is famous for its frescos of *Law Through the Ages* but the later murals in the Jury Assembly Room are works with which potential jurors become very, very familiar while waiting to fulfill their civic duty.

NEW COURT HOUSE, NEW YORK CITY.

ROCKEFELLER CENTER

The ovular building pictured here was part of the original plan for Rockefeller Center but fortunately was scrapped. The area now contains the two smaller rectangular buildings—the British Empire Building and La Maison Francaise—and between them the Channel Gardens, which pay homage to the first public botanical garden on that site. These gardens add to the visual splendor of the focal point of the Center—the 850-foot RCA Building—and help to create one of the truly magnificent outdoor public spaces in the city.

FUTURE NEW YORK, "THE CITY OF SKYSCRAPERS"

This fun postcard gives a glimpse of one person's view of the future of the city. In 1932, Edward Bellemy made predictions for New York City in the year 1982. He surmised that the population would reach 50 million, absorbing Long Island, White Plains, and Yonkers; that the East River would be filled in; that 200- to 250-story buildings would be the norm; and that roadways would be tiered, elevated structures, sometimes passing right through buildings. The inhabitants of this city would subsist on concentrates, pellets, and pills, making restaurants and cafes passé, and women would give up on skirts altogether and wear something akin to bathing suits. This population would be sustained by an eternal life serum invented by a high school genius, which would keep such greats as Will Rogers and Calvin Coolidge alive!

NEW YORK IN THE FUTURE.

GLOBE TOWER, CONEY ISLAND

In 1906, Sam Friede announced plans to build this 700-foot Globe
Tower at Coney Island. It was to contain a vaudeville theater, an aer-
ial hippodrome, a five-ring circus, a revolving restaurant, a hotel, an
observatory, and even a telegraph station! The funds for the project
were never raised, and it was later determined to be a hoax.

BIBLIOGRAPHY

Ashley, Diana. *Where to Dine in Thirty-nine: A Guide to New York Restaurants, to Which There Is Added a Cook Book of Recipes by Famous Chefs.* New York: Crown Publishers, 1939.

Aylesworth, Thomas G., and Virginia L. *New York, the Glamour Years (1919–1945).* New York: Gallery Books, 1987.

Beard, Rick, and Leslie Cohen Berlowitz. *Greenwich Village: Culture and Counterculture.* New Brunswick, New Jersey: Rutgers University Press, 1993.

Batterberry, Michael and Ariane. *On the Town in New York: The Landmark History of Eating, Drinking, and Entertainments from the American Revolution to the Food Revolution.* New York: Routledge Press, 1999.

Bloom, Ken. *Broadway: An Encyclopedic Guide to the History, People, and Places of Times Square.* New York: Facts on File, 1991.

Bunyan, Patrick. *All Around the Town: Amazing Manhattan Facts and Curiosities.* New York: Fordham University Press, 1999.

Cudany, Brian J. *Around Manhattan Island and Other Maritime Tales of New York.* New York: Fordham University Press, 1997.

Chase, W. Parker. *New York, the Wonder City.* New York: Wonder City Publishing Co., 1931.

Gabrielan, Randall. *Brooklyn New York in Vintage Postcards.* Charleston, South Carolina: Arcadia Publishing, 1999.

———. *New York City's Financial District in Vintage Postcards.* Charleston, South Carolina: Arcadia Publishing, 2000.

———. *Times Square and 42nd Street in Vintage Postcards.* Charleston, South Carolina: Arcadia Publishing, 2000.

Gershman, Michael. *Diamonds: The Evolution of the Ballpark.* Boston: Houghton Mifflin, 1993.

Gold, Joyce. *From Windmills to the World Trade Center: A Walking Guide to Lower Manhattan History.* New York: Old Warren Road Press, 1982.

Goldston, Harmoin H., with Martha Dalrymple. *History Preserved: A Guide to New York City Landmarks and Historic Districts.* New York: Simon and Schuster, 1974.

The Great East River Bridge, 1883–1983. New York: Brooklyn Museum/Harry N. Abrams, 1983.

Homberger, Eric. *The Historical Atlas of New York City.* New York: Henry Holt & Co., 1994.

Jackson, Kenneth T., ed. *The Encyclopedia of New York City.* New Haven: Yale University Press/New York Historical Society, 1995.

Kannapell, Andrea, ed., and the Editors of the *New York Times's* Popular "FYI" Column (Editor). *The Curious New Yorker.* New York: Times Books, 1999.

King's Handbook of New York City, 1893. New York: Benjamin Blom Inc., 1972, reissue.

Knopf Guides: New York. New York: Alfred A. Knopf, 1994.

Lockwood, Charles. *Manhattan Moves Uptown.* Boston: Houghton Mifflin Company, 1976.

Lowry, Philip J. *Green Cathedrals: The Ultimate Celebration of All 271 Major League and Negro League Ballparks Past and Present.* Reading, Massachusetts: Addison-Wesley Publishing Company, 1992.

Middleton, Scudder. *Dining, Wining and Dancing in New York*. New York: Dodge Publishing Company, 1938.

Morrone, Francis. *The Architectural Guidebook to New York City*. Salt Lake City: Gibbs Smith, Publisher, 1998.

Moscow, Henry. *The Book of New York Firsts*. New York: Macmillan, 1982.

Patterson, Jerry E. *Fifth Avenue: The Best Address*. New York: Rizzoli, 1998.

Rector, George. *Dining in New York with Rector: A Personal Guide to Good Eating*. New York: Prentice-Hall, Inc., 1939.

Reidenbaugh, Lowell. *The Sporting News Take Me Out to the Ball Park*, rev. 2nd edn. St. Louis, Missouri: Sporting News Publishing Company, 1987.

Ritter, Lawrence S. *Lost Ballparks: A Celebration of Baseball's Legendary Fields*. New York: Viking Studio Books, 1992.

Ross, George. *Tips on Tables: Being a Guide to Dining and Wining in New York at 365 Restaurants Suitable to Every Mood and Every Purse*. New York: Covici, Friede Publishers, 1934.

Salwen, Peter. *Upper West Side Story: A History and Guide*. New York: Abbeville Press, 1989.

Schoener, Allon. *Harlem on My Mind: Cultural Capital of Black America, 1900–1968*. New York: New Press, 1995.

Schwartz, David, Steve Ryan, and Fred Wostbrock. *The Encyclopedia of TV Game Shows*. New York: Facts on File, Inc., 1999.

Silver, Nathan. *Lost New York,,* expanded and updated edn. Boston: Houghton Mifflin, 2000.

Smith, Jack H. *Old New York in Picture Postcards, 1900–1945*. Lanham, Maryland: Vestal Press, 1999.

Stallworth, Lyn, and Rod Kennedy Jr. *The Brooklyn Cookbook*. New York: Knopf, 1991.

Stern, Robert A. M. *New York 1880, 1900, 1930, 1960*, four vols. New York: Rizzoli, 1983–1999.

Tucker, Kerry. *Greetings from New York: A Visit to Manhattan in Postcards*. New York: Delilah Books, 1981.

Walker, Danton. *Guide to New York Nitelife*. New York: Putnam, 1958.

White, Norval, and Elliot Willensky. *AIA Guide to New York City*, fourth ed. New York: Harcourt Brace Jovanovich, 2000.

Willensky, Elliot. *When Brooklyn Was the World, 1920–1957*. New York: Harmony Books, 1986.

Wolfe, Gerard R. *New York: A Guide to the Metropoli*. New York: McGraw Hill, 1994.

The WPA Guide to New York City: The Federal Writers Project Guide to 1930's New York. New York: The New Press, 1992.

Wright, Carol von Pressentin. *Blue Guide New York*. New York: W. W. Norton, 1991.

Wright, Susan. *New York City in Photographs 1850–1945*. New York: Barnes & Noble Books, 1999.

Zaid, Barry. *Wish You Were Here: A Tour of America's Great Hotels During the Golden Age of the Picture Post Card*. New York: Crown Publishers, 1990.

INDEX

Abyssinian Baptist Church, 54
Academy of Music, 68
Adams Chewing Gum, 59
Adams, Reverend James B., 54
Alhambra Theatre, 51
Allyson, June, 62
America (theatrical production), 67
American Museum of Natural History, 77
Ammann, Othmar H., 97
Amsterdam Avenue, 51
Apollo, the, 50
Apple Tours, 75
Arabian Nights Ball, 26
Armstrong, Louis, 50
Astor, Caroline Schermerhorn, 38
Astor, William Waldorf, 38
Audubon Theatre, 50
Automat, 94
Autopiano Company, the, 48
Bailey, Mildred, 50
Baker, Carroll, 62
Baker, Josephine, 50
Bank of Manhattan Building, 81
Barnum, P.T., 78
Basie, Count, 50
Battery Park, 16
Bayard Street, 21
Bellemy, Edward, 99
Bellevue Hospital, 45
Belmont Hotel, 42
Belmont, August, 80
Bergdorf-Goodman, 46
Berle, Milton, 60
Berlin, Irving, 20
Bernhardt, Sarah, 28
Billingsley, Sherman, 62
Biltmore Hotel, 42
Black, Leonard, 54
Blackmer, Sydney, 68
Blackwell's Island, 45
Bliss, Lillie P., 76
Bloomingdale Insane Asylum, 48
Bogart, Humphrey, 62
Bonaparte, Joseph, 49
Bonaparte, Napoleon, 49
Bond Clothing Store, 37
Brady, "Diamond Jim," 47
Brecker, Louis, 63
"Bridge of Sighs," 19
Broadway, 18, 25, 27, 32, 35, 39, 48, 50, 63, 67, 68
Bronx Zoo, 16, 52
Bronx, the, 52-53, 98
Brooklyn Bridge, 54, 58, 78
Brooklyn Dodgers, 70
Brooklyn Heights, 55
Brooklyn Navy Yard, 57
Brooklyn, 54-57
Burr, Aaron, 78
Byrd, Admiral Richard E., 85
Calloway, Cab, 50
Canarsee Indians, 57
Carpathia (ship), 15
Castle Clinton, 16
Castle Garden, 16
Cathedral of St. John the Divine, 48, 82
Central Park West, 48
Central Park, 46-47, 77
Central Theatre, 40
Centre Street, 19
Chang, Li Hung, 21
Chelsea Piers, 15
Chinatown, 21
Chop Suey, 21
Chrysler Building, 81
Circle Line, 74
City Hall Park, 19, 96
City Hall Station (subway), 82
City Investing Building, 18
Claremont Inn, 49
Club 18, 63

Cole, Nat King, 62
Columbia University, 48
Columbus Avenue, 90
Columbus Circle, 48
Columbus Park, 21
Columbus, Christopher, 48
Concord Baptist Church of Christ, 54
Coney Island, 16, 25, 55, 65, 81, 100
Connie's Inn, 50
Coolidge, Calvin, 99
Copacabana, 62
Corps de Ballet, 69
Corrigan, Douglas "Wrongway," 85
Cortlandt Street, 18
Cotton Club , 50
Crabbe, Buster, 55
Criminal Courts Building, 19
Dahl, Arlene, 60
Darin, Bobby, 62
Davis, John W., 26
Dekalb Avenue, 54
Delmonico's, 64
Democratic National Convention, 26
Dempsey, Jack, 66
Dickens, Charles, 45
Dimaggio, Joe, 71
Duchamp, Marcel, 27
Dunn, Arty, 60
Durante, Jimmy, 20, 62
E.J. Clark Carpet Shop, 58
Earhart, Amelia, 85
East River, 45
Ebbets Field, 70
Elevated railroad, 41, 82
Ellington, Duke, 50
Ellis Island, 14, 16
Empire State Building, 38, 81
Eveready, 59
Fairbanks, Douglas, 67
Faller, Hank, 62
Famous Hollywood Cabaret, 63
Fanny Farmer Candies, 90
Farmer, Fanny Merrit, 90
Faust (opera), 68
Federal Hall National Memorial, 17
Feltman's (restaurant), 65
Feltman, Charles, 65
Fifth Avenue Coach Company, 39
Fifth Avenue, 25, 38, 40
Financial District, 17-19
Fitzgerald, Ella, 50, 62
Flagg, Ernest T., 18, 80
Flagg, James Montgomery, 66
Flatbush Avenue, 54
Flatiron Building, 25
Floyd Bennett Field, 85
Foley Square, 98
Fraunces Tavern, 17
Freed, Alan, 54
Freedlander, Joseph H., 39
French, Daniel Chester, 26
Friede, Sam, 100
Friedgen's Drugstore, 51
Friedgen, Charles, 51
Fuchs, Sammy, 22
Fulton, Robert, 78
Gae Foster Roxyettes, 68
GE Building, 41
Gehrig, Lou, 71
General Post Office, 96
George Washington Bridge, 97
Gershwin, George, 20, 69
Gershwin, Ira, 20
Giants Stadium, 70
Gilbert, Cass, 81, 97
Gilmore Gardens, 25
Gimbel Brothers, 30
Giuliani, Mayor Rudolph, 75
Gleason, Jackie, 62
Godfrey, Arthur, 63
Goethals Bridge, 59

Governor's Island, 14
Grand Central Terminal, 43, 44, 94
Grand Concourse, 53
Granlund, Nils T., 63
Grant's Tomb, 14, 51, 96
Grant, General Ulysses S., 96
Gravesend, 57
Gray Line, 75
Greenbelt, the, 73
Gude, O. J., 36
Guggenheim Museum, 76
Guggenheim, Solomon R., 76
Gulf and Western Plaza, 48
Hamilton, Alexander, 17, 78
Hampton, Lionel, 50
Harlem, 50-51
Hatari (movie), 54
Heins & La Farge, 48
Helleu, Paul, 43
Heyward, DuBose, 69
Hippodrome, the, 67
Hogan, Michael, 49
Holland Tunnel, 84, 95
Holland, Clifford M., 84
Horace Harding Boulevard, 73
Horn & Hardart, 94
Horne, Lena, 50
Hotel Astor, 36
Hotel Bristol, 93
Hotel Chelsea, 28
Hotel Commodore, 42
Hotel Concourse Plaza, 53
Hotel Dixie, 62
Hotel Lexington, 63
Hotel Pennsylvania, 29
Hotel Piccadilly, 60
Hotel Sheraton, 62
Hotel St. George, 55
Hotel Victoria, 92
Hubbell, Carl, 70
Hudson River, 48, 49
Hudson Tunnel, 84
Hudson-Fulton Celebration, 14
Hughes, Howard, 85
Iceland Skating Rink, 72
Ingalls, Laura, 85
International Casino, 36
International Design Center, 59
Iona, Andy, 63
Irving Place, 68
Jack Dempsey's Restaurant, 66
Kandinsky, Wassily, 76
Kennedy, Frank, 60
Kidd, Captain, 17
Kingsbridge Road, 52
Kinney, Ray, 63
Klee, Paul, 76
Kodak Colorama, 43
Krupa, Gene, 50
LaGuardia Airport, 85
Landmarks Preservation Commission, 29
Lane, Tony, 62
Latin Quarter, 60-61
Lawrence, Captain George, 78
Lee, Bradford Gilbert, 78
Leigh, Douglas, 37
Lenox Avenue, 50
Lever Building, 44
Lewis, Joe E., 62
Lexington Avenue, 62
Liberty Plaza, 18
Lincoln Center, 68
Lincoln Tunnel, 84
Lindbergh, Charles, 85
London Dog and Bird Shop, 38
Long Island City, 59
Long Island University, 54
Loose-Wiles Sunshine Biscuit Company, 59
Lowell, Guy, 98
Lower East Side, 20-23, 51
Lusitania (ship), 15

Macy's, 30
Macy, R.H., 30
Madison Square Garden, 25, 26, 71, 72
Madison Square, 18, 25-26, 80
Majestic Theatre, 69
Manhattan Bridge, 23
Manhattan Cocktail (movie), 54
Mantle, Mickey, 71
Martin Beck Theatre, 68
Marx Brothers, 20
Marx, Groucho, 96
Mayes, Willie, 70
McClellan, Mayor George B., 82
McGoldrick Mercury Motors, 58
McGraw, John J., 70
McKim, Charles, 29
Metropolitan Life Insurance Building, 18, 25, 44, 80
Metropolitan Life Insurance Company, 25, 81
Metropolitan Museum of Art, 77
Metropolitan Opera House, 68
Midland Beach, 59
Miller, Arthur, 28
Miller, Glen, 29
Miranda, Carmen, 62
A Modern Musketeer (movie), 67
Monroe, Marilyn, 28
Moses, (Grandma) Anna Mary Robertson , 30
Moses, Robert, 23
Mott Street, 21
Mould, Jacob Wrey, 77
Mulberry Bend Park, 21
Mulberry Bend, 21
Municipal Building, 19
Muris, Roger, 71
Museum of Modern Art, 76
National Airlines, 14
National League Baseball Park, 70
NBC Studios, 92
Nesbit, Evelyn, 25
Nevins Brothers, 60
New Murray Hill Hotel, 42
New Year's Eve, 32
New York and Harlem Railroad, 25
New York Aquarium, 16
New York Central Building, 44
New York County Courthouse, 98
New York Giants (baseball team), 70
New York Giants (football team), 70
New York Harbor, 13-14, 75
New York Jets, 70
New York Knicks, 71
New York Life Insurance Building, 26
New York Rangers, 71
New York State Supreme Court, 98
New York Stock Exchange, 17
New York Telegram, 80
New York Times, 32
New York Tribune, 32
New York World's Fair (1939), 55, 58, 85, 86-89, 92
New York World's Fair (1964), 70
New York World Building, 19
New York Yankees, 70
New York Zoological Park, 52
Newark Airport, 85
Newman, Paul, 68
Newspaper Row, 19, 32
Nino's Ten East, 66
Normandie (ship), 13
Northern Boulevard, 58
O'Dwyer, Mayor William, 22
O'Henry, 28
O'Malley, Walter, 70
Ochs, Aldoph, 32
Otis, Elisha G., 78
Ott, Met, 70
Outerbridge Crossing, 59
Paddy's Clamhouse, 64

Page, Geraldine, 68
Pan Am Building, 44
Paramount Theater, 54
Park Avenue, 44, 94
Park Row Building, 80
Park Row, 19, 80
Park Street, 21
Parkchester, 53
Pennsylvania Station, 29, 71
Pershing Square, 42
Piccadilly Circus Bar, 60
Plantation Club, 50
Planter's Peanuts, 34-35
Plaza Hotel, 46
Poe Cottage, 52
Poe, Edgar Allen, 52
Pollock, Jackson, 28
Polo Grounds, 70, 98
Porgy & Bess (opera), 69
Port Authority Bus Terminal, 84
Port Authority Trans-Hudson Corporation (PATH), 84
Port of New York Authority, 84
Post, George B., 80
Potter Building, 19
Prescott, Linzee, 66
Pulitzer Building, 80
Pulitzer, Joseph B., 80
Pullman car, 82
Queen Elizabeth (ship), 13
Queen Mary (ship), 13
Queens Boulevard, 73
Queens Roller Rink, 73
Queens, 58-59, 66, 73, 85, 86
Quiz Kids (television program), 92
Radio City Music Hall, 40, 68, 69
Rainbow Room, 41
RCA Building, 40, 41
Recreation Pier, 72
Reuben's Restaurant, 66
Reuben, Arnold, 66
Reynolds, William H., 81
Rickard, Tex, 71
Riis, Jacob, 21
Ritz Tower Building, 96
Ritz-Carlton Hotel, 96
Riverside Drive, 49
Rivoli Theater, 67
Robinson, Jackie, 70
Rockaway Beach Amusement Park, 58
Rockaway Beach, 58
Rockefeller Center, 40-41, 68, 69, 92, 99
Rockefeller, Abbie Aldrich, 76
Rockettes, 68, 69
Rogers, Will, 99
Roosevelt Island, 45
Roseland Ballroom, 63
Roseland Dance City, 63
Rothafel, Samuel L. "Roxy," 67, 68, 69
Roxy Theater, 68
Royal Blue Line, 75
Rudy & Maxli's Brau-Haus, 65
Russell, Lillian, 28, 47
Russian Bear (restaurant), 64
Ruth, Babe, 70, 71
Sammy's Original Bowery Cabaret, 22
Savoy Ballroom, 50
Schwab, Charles, 49
Seagram Building, 44
Severance, H. Craig, 81
Shea Stadium, 70
Siegel-Cooper Department Store, 26
Silver Cup Studios, 59
Sinatra, Frank, 60, 62
Singer Building, 18, 80
Singer Sewing Machine Company, 18
Sloan, John, 27, 28
Small's Paradise, 50
Smith, Al, 20, 26

Sofia Brothers Warehouse, 90
St. George Ferry, 59
St. Luke's Episcopal Church, 74
Staten Island, 59, 73, 75
Staten Island Ferry, 59, 75
Statue of Liberty, 13, 16
Stork Club, 62
Strauss, Isador, 30
Strauss, Nathan, 30
Stuyvesant, Peter, 17
Subway, 82
Sullivan, Mary Quinn, 76
Sun Building, 19
Sweet Bird of Youth (play), 68
Thaw, Harry K., 25
Thomas, Dylan, 28
Thompson Avenue, 59
Tichenor Riding School, 48
Times Building, 19, 32
Times Square, 32-37, 51
Titanic (ship), 15, 28
Todt Hill, 73
Tombs, the, 19
Torn, Rip, 68
Traffic towers, 39
Tribune Building, 19
Trinity Church, 32, 78
Trotsky, Leon, 64
Trump International Plaza, 48
Tucker, Sophie, 60
Twain, Mark, 28
Tweed, "Boss," 45
U.S. Coast Guard, 85
U.S. Navy, 48, 85
Underhill, Irving, 96
Union Square, 27
United Nations, 45
Upjohn, Richard, 78
Upper West Side, 48-49
Van Allan, William, 81
Vanderbilt Hotel, 94
Vaudeville, 22, 32, 51, 60
Vaughan, Sarah, 50
Vaux, Calvert, 77
Vernon, Irene, 60
Verrazano, Giovanni da, 13
Waldorf-Astoria Hotel, 38
Walker, Mayor Jimmie, 50
Wall Street, 17
Walter, Barbara, 60
Walters, Lou, 60
Washington Arch, 27
Washington Square, 27, 39
Washington, George, 17, 27, 96
Waters, Ethel, 50
Wayne, John, 54
Weismantel's Showboat, 66
Weissmuller, Johnny, 55
Welfare Island, 45
West Side Highway, 49
West, Mae, 45, 60
White, Jack, 63
White, Patrick, 64
White, Samson, 54
White, Stanford, 25
William, Prince, 49
Williams, Tennessee, 28, 68
Williamsburg Bridge, 23
Williamsbridge Road, 53
Willis Avenue, 58
Wilson Line, 74
Wilson, Julie, 60
Wiman, Erastus, 59
Winchell, Walter, 62
WINS (radio station), 54
Wolfe, Thomas, 28
Woolworth Building, 80
World Building, 80, 82